IXL SUMMER WORKBOOK

THE ULTIMATE SUMMER WORKBOOK

FOR THE SUMMER BETWEEN GRADES 3 & 4

© 2025 IXL Learning. All rights reserved. No part of this publication may be reproduced transmitted, in any form or by any means (electronic, mechanical, photocopying, recor prior written permission of IXL Learning.

ISBN: 978-1-964670-06-5
29 28 27 26 25 1 2 3 4 5

Printed in the USA

About this book

Keep your child engaged with learning over summer break with the Ultimate IXL Summer Workbook! The activities in this workbook are perfect for reinforcing key skills from the past year and building new skills in preparation for the year ahead.

DAILY PRACTICE

This workbook contains 60 days of activities. Each day consists of 2 full pages of activities that can be completed in about 15 minutes. At 5 days per week, this workbook is perfect for a 12-week summer break! Throughout the week, your child will engage in math and language arts activities, complete a science or social studies page, and wrap up with enrichment activities.

BRAIN BREAKS

Brain breaks are sprinkled throughout. These fun breaks include physical and sensory activities.

 **Brain Break!** Take ten baby steps. Then take ten giant steps. Now, try walking on your heels or on your toes. Can you go backwards?

ACTIVITY TRACKER

Track your child's progress with the activity tracker! Have your child color in the bubble or cover it with a sticker after completing each day's work. Watch as the tracker fills up throughout the summer!

CERTIFICATE OF COMPLETION

Found at the back of the book, the certificate of completion is a great way to help you recognize your child's hard work!

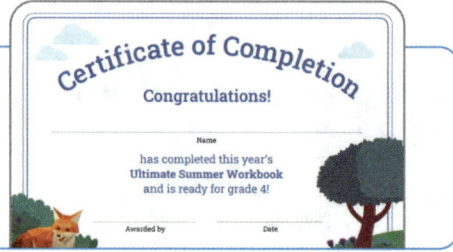

 **Materials:** To complete this workbook, your child will need a pencil and crayons or colored pencils.

Continue the fun with IXL.com!

Throughout the book, look for these IXL.com skill IDs. For additional practice, go to the website or the IXL mobile app and enter the three-digit code into the search bar.

IXL.com skill ID
N2M

IXL provides all the tools your child needs to succeed.

LIMITLESS LEARNING

Unlock your child's full potential with access to 17,000 engaging units in math, English, science, social studies, and Spanish. With examples and 1,300 video lessons across all grade levels, your learner can review a concept before diving into a skill.

PERSONALIZED PLAN

IXL's Diagnostic pinpoints your child's knowledge level and creates a customized plan to boost achievement.

REAL-TIME FEEDBACK

Detailed explanations after missed questions allow your child to learn from mistakes and work toward achieving mastery.

AWARDS AND CERTIFICATES

Whimsical awards and certificates help you celebrate your child and keep motivation high.

EDUCATIONAL GAMES

Fun-filled games provide hands-on practice in essential concepts and help your child develop a love of learning.

20% off For a limited time, receive 20% off your IXL family membership. Visit **www.ixl.com/workbook/34s** or scan the **QR code** for details.

Activity tracker

Keep track of your progress! Color in the bubble or cover it with a sticker after you complete each day's work.

Week 1
Days 1–5
① ② ③ ④ ⑤

Week 2
Days 6–10
⑥ ⑦ ⑧ ⑨ ⑩

Week 3
Days 11–15
⑪ ⑫ ⑬ ⑭ ⑮

Week 4
Days 16–20
⑯ ⑰ ⑱ ⑲ ⑳

Week 5
Days 21–25
㉑ ㉒ ㉓ ㉔ ㉕

Week 6
Days 26–30
㉖ ㉗ ㉘ ㉙ ㉚

Week 7
Days 31–35
㉛ ㉜ ㉝ ㉞ ㉟

Week 8
Days 36–40
㊱ ㊲ ㊳ ㊴ ㊵

Week 9
Days 41–45
㊶ ㊷ ㊸ ㊹ ㊺

Week 10
Days 46–50
㊻ ㊼ ㊽ ㊾ ㊿

Week 11
Days 51–55
51 52 53 54 55

Week 12
Days 56–60
56 57 58 59 60

Weeks 1–3: Overview

Week 1

Math
Addition and subtraction within 1,000
Place value

Social studies
Reading a map

Language arts
Synonyms and antonyms
Opinions and reasons
Making inferences in a story

Enrichment
Logic puzzle
Word categories

Week 2

Math
Number sequences
Expanded form

Science
Photosynthesis

Language arts
Prefixes and suffixes
Topic sentences
Main idea of a passage

Enrichment
Drawing challenge
Scavenger hunt

Week 3

Math
Addition and subtraction within 10,000
Modeling fractions

Social studies
Government

Language arts
Understanding characters
Shades of meaning
Figurative language

Enrichment
Sudoku
Multiple-meaning words

More ways to learn

Keep the learning going! Summer is the perfect time to explore, learn, and have fun. Use these simple, exciting activities to help you stay active, curious, and creative during your summer break.

See how many activities you can do! Cross off each activity as you complete it.

Make up your own theme song. 	**Gather items to donate to charity.** 	**Draw a self-portrait.** 
Write a poem. 	**Build a tower or castle with household items.** 	**Go on a hike.** 
Play "Would You Rather" with someone. 	**Read to a friend or family member.** 	**Make a list of your favorite things.** 

DAY 1: Add and subtract within 1,000

IXL.com skill ID **2TD**

Add or subtract.

```
  413        653        982
+ 572      - 421      - 645


  408        293        842
+ 293      -  58      +  95


  153        809        169
+ 729      - 762      + 514
```

Write each missing digit.

```
   9 9 ▢        ▢ 3 6        9 5 ▢
 - 1 ▢ 6      + 4 8 ▢      - ▢ 5 6
 -------      -------      -------
   8 6 1        8 1 8        3 9 8


   5 8 ▢        8 1 ▢        1 ▢ 7
 + ▢ 1 5      - 3 ▢ 4      + 6 7 ▢
 -------      -------      -------
   8 0 1        5 0 9        8 2 3
```

Exclusive offer! For a limited time, receive 20% off your IXL family membership. Scan this QR code or visit www.ixl.com/workbook/34s for details.

MATH

DAY 1: Synonyms and antonyms

IXL.com skill ID **N2M**

Solve the crossword puzzle.

- All of the across answers are **antonyms** of the clues.
- All of the down answers are **synonyms** of the clues.

2 across: I N S I D E

Across – Antonyms

2. Outside
6. Weak
7. Cry
8. Asleep
10. Same
13. Never
14. Messy

Down – Synonyms

1. End
3. Toss
4. Frightened
5. Journey
9. Middle
11. Quick
12. Story

DAY 2: Opinions and reasons

IXL.com skill ID **CXD**

Read each opinion statement below. Then put an X next to the reason that best supports the opinion.

| Car trips are a fun way to travel. | ____ Cruise ships have swimming pools and games.
____ Some people get bored during long car rides.
____ When driving, you are free to stop and look around. |

| Strawberries are the easiest fruit to grow at home. | ____ Strawberries are sweet, bright red, and heart shaped.
____ Strawberries can be grown in pots or in the ground.
____ Strawberries need at least eight hours of sun each day. |

| You should always bring a hat when you go hiking. | ____ It's fun to wear a hat that shows your favorite team.
____ Hats can help protect you from the sun.
____ If you have a lot to carry, a hat might be hard to pack. |

| Bikers should not wear headphones while biking. | ____ Headphones make it harder to hear nearby traffic.
____ Some headphones can be worn with helmets.
____ Headphones allow bikers to listen to music as they ride. |

Brain Break! Stand up. Bring your left knee up and touch it with your right elbow. Then bring your right knee up and touch it with your left elbow. Do this for a count of twenty!

DAY 2 Place value

Answer each question using one of the numbers in the box. Some numbers will not be used.

> 508   475   983
> 624
>   206
> 348   129
>   133
>   710
> 919   862   557

I have an 8 in the tens place. What number am I? _____

I have a digit with a value of 300. What number am I? _____

I have a 6 in the ones place. What number am I? _____

I have a digit with a value of 70. What number am I? _____

I have 2 more hundreds than ones. What number am I? _____

I have 7 fewer tens than ones. What number am I? _____

I have only even digits that add up to 16. What number am I? _____

I have the same digit in both the tens place and the ones place. What number am I? _____

DAY 3: Reading comprehension

Read the first part of the story. Then answer the questions.

A Puzzling Surprise

Emma and her father walked down the crowded sidewalk at the Fairview Summer Festival. The sun had been shining brightly all morning, and Emma's face was beginning to feel warm.

"Let's see if we can find some place inside to cool off," said Emma's father.

Emma looked over toward the buildings and noticed a big sign that read "Jigsaw Puzzle Contest." She pointed to it. "Can we check it out, Dad?" Emma asked. She and her dad had lots of puzzles at home, so she was curious to see what awaited them inside.

The cool air was a welcome relief as they walked into a large room. It was crowded with teams of people standing around tables. The room was filled with a mix of adults and kids, some even younger than Emma. The air buzzed, and all eyes were on the small boxes wrapped in brown paper at the center of each table.

All of a sudden, an announcer's voice boomed through the room. "All right, puzzlers! Ready, set, begin!"

How do the people in the room most likely feel? How do you know?

_____

_____

Which sentence is most likely true? Put an X next to the correct answer.

____ Emma has never been to a jigsaw puzzle contest before.

____ Emma comes to the jigsaw puzzle contest every year.

____ Emma doesn't like jigsaw puzzles.

DAY 3 Reading comprehension

Read the next part of the story and answer the questions. Put an X next to the correct answer.

> There was a rustling sound as the people at the tables unwrapped their boxes and started sorting puzzle pieces. A large clock on the wall counted the minutes as the teams raced to complete their puzzles.
>
> Emma and her dad walked around the room, quietly watching the teams work. Hands were **flying** across the tables, moving pieces into place at lightning speed. After about thirty minutes, the people on one team shouted and raised their hands. They had won the contest! There were a few claps, but the rest of the teams continued their puzzles. Emma thought they must be having too much fun to stop.
>
> "So what do you think, kiddo?" Emma's dad asked her cheerfully.
>
> "This is so cool! We need to start practicing now if we want to have a chance at next year's puzzle contest," Emma said with a grin.

What is the meaning of **flying** in the second paragraph above?

____ soaring through the sky

____ moving quickly

____ flapping in the wind

Based on the story, which sentence is most likely true?

____ Emma and her dad like to do jigsaw puzzles together.

____ Emma's dad likes jigsaw puzzles more than Emma does.

____ Emma and her dad wish that they had stayed home.

Which word best describes how Emma feels at the end of the story?

____ bored   ____ confused   ____ eager   ____ shy

DAY 4: Word problems

Splash Town Water Park is open for the summer! Answer each question.

The Quiet Creek Lazy River has big tubes and small tubes. There are 375 big tubes and 260 small tubes. How many tubes are there in all?

_____ tubes

Splash Town has two new water slides this year, Splash Summit and Hydro Heights. Splash Summit is 319 feet long. Hydro Heights is 145 feet long. How much longer is Splash Summit than Hydro Heights?

_____ feet longer

The park has 950 lockers for rent. If 416 lockers are in use, how many lockers are not in use?

_____ lockers

When Splash Town opens, 729 visitors enter the park. During the day, 236 visitors leave and 478 visitors enter the park. How many visitors are at the water park at the end of the day?

_____ visitors

There are 500 lounge chairs around the Aqua Oasis Pool. If 137 adults and 204 children are currently sitting in chairs, how many chairs are open?

_____ chairs

DAY 4 — Read a map

Evan is traveling around Belford Island. Read the clues and use the map to learn where he stopped along the way. Write the answers on the lines.

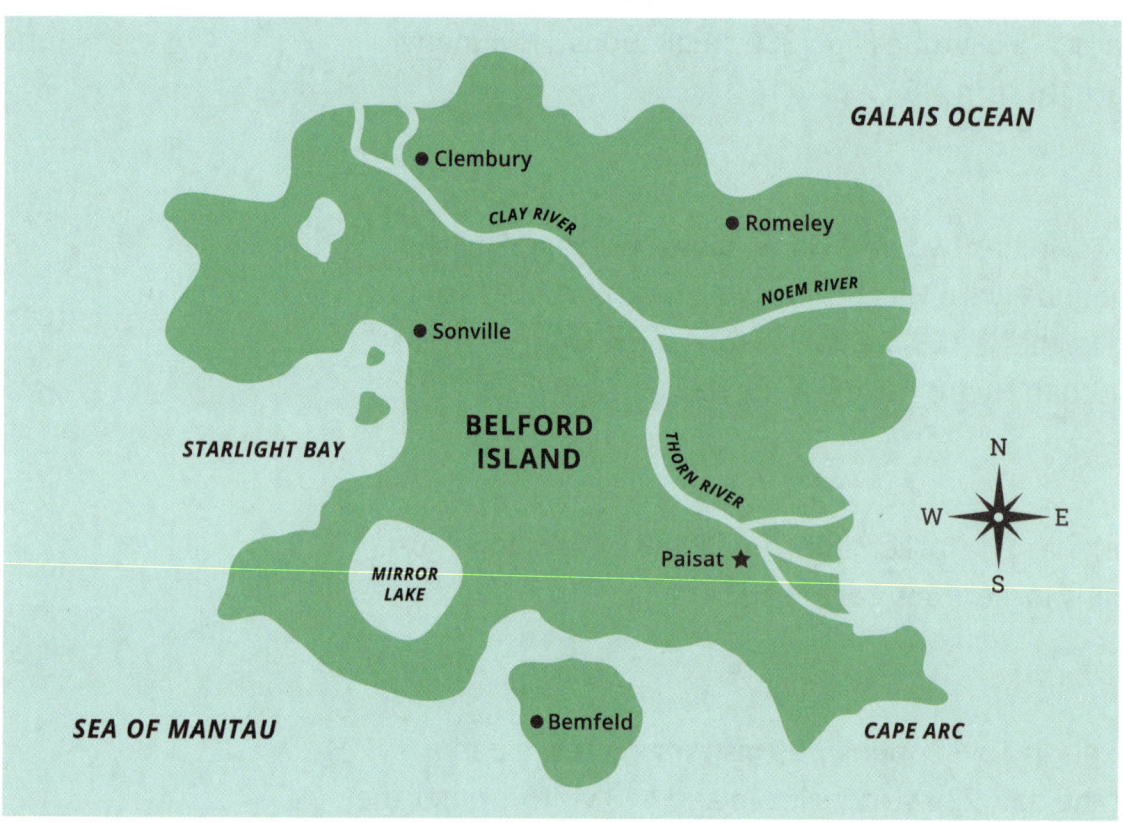

Evan started his journey at this city next to the Clay River. _____

Then, he traveled south to this city on the Starlight Bay. _____

Next, he went east to where the Clay River splits into these two rivers. _____

Then, Evan traveled southeast along the Thorn River to this capital city. _____

Finally, he took a boat to this city on an island in the Sea of Mantau. _____

DAY 5 Logic puzzle

The families in the Springview neighborhood are planning their summer vacations. Each family is going to a different place.

Use the clues and the grid below to discover where each family is going on vacation.

- None of the families are going to a place that begins with the same letter as their name.
- The Morales family, the Chen family, and the Harris family don't like sand, so they are not going to the beach.
- The Morales family and the Chen family went to Historic Huntstown last year, so they aren't going again this year.
- The Harris family is looking forward to lots of thrill rides on their vacation.

	Places				
Families	Briney Beach	Mirabella Mountains	Celia City	Thenway Theme Park	Historic Huntstown
Morales family					
Baker family					
Chen family					
Taylor family					
Harris family					

DAY 5: Word categories

Sort the words into categories to solve the puzzle. Each category will contain three words. Each word will be used in only one category.

pause	wow	airplane	kayak	amazing
wonderful	great	brake	boat	handlebar
pedal	rest	car	wheel	level

Category	Word 1	Word 2	Word 3
Words spelled the same backward and forward			
Words to express a job well done			
Words that mean "to stop"			
Parts of a bike			
Ways to travel			

DAY 6 — Number sequences

Write the missing numbers to complete each sequence.

| 57 | 67 | 77 | | 97 | | |

| 78 | | | 81 | 82 | 83 | |

| 220 | | 420 | 520 | | 720 | |

| 1,154 | 1,155 | | 1,157 | 1,158 | | |

| 600 | 1,600 | 2,600 | | | | |

| 4,752 | 4,852 | | 5,052 | 5,152 | | |

| 1,996 | 1,997 | 1,998 | | | 2,001 | |

DAY 6: Prefixes and suffixes

IXL.com skill ID **LDS**

Look at the words in the design below. Each word has a prefix or a suffix. On the blanks, write the prefix or suffix that matches the meaning. Then color the design using the key.

- **RED** — before: _pre-_
- **ORANGE** — again: _____
- **YELLOW** — incorrectly: _____
- **GREEN** — can be done: _____
- **BLUE** — full of: _____
- **PURPLE** — without: _____

18

DAY 7: Expanded form

Add to show each number in standard form.

5,000 + 700 + 20 + 6 = _____

6,000 + 200 + 30 + 1 = _____

2,000 + 900 + 40 + 3 = _____

5,000 + 400 + 60 + 5 = _____

8,000 + 100 + 50 + 4 = _____

1,000 + 70 + 8 = _____

3,000 + 600 + 10 + 7 = _____

4,000 + 800 + 9 = _____

Write the missing numbers to show each number in expanded form.

4,836 = 4,000 + _____ + 30 + _____

8,765 = _____ + 700 + 60 + _____

1,694 = 1,000 + 600 + _____ + _____

3,953 = 3,000 + _____ + _____ + 3

6,522 = 6,000 + _____ + 20 + _____

2,381 = _____ + _____ + _____ + 1

5,714 = _____ + _____ + 10 + _____

9,299 = _____ + 200 + _____ + _____

Brain Break! Sit up straight in a chair or on the floor. Put one hand over your heart, and rest the other on your belly. Breathe in deeply through your nose and feel your chest and belly fill with air. Then slowly breathe out through your nose. Repeat this five times.

DAY 7: Topic sentences

IXL.com skill ID **GHA**

A **topic sentence** tells the reader the main idea of a paragraph.

Draw lines to match each topic sentence on the left with the **two** details that best support it.

Parks are an important part of a city or town.

There are many ways to enjoy an afternoon outdoors at the park.

Parks are just one place you can have a picnic.

Some people like flying kites or playing ball.

In Alaska, you can have a picnic on a snowy glacier.

Many parks offer classes and camps for children who attend local schools.

Many towns hold special events and festivals at local parks.

People also picnic on top of waterfalls and in hot air balloons.

Some people enjoy walking along a nature path or napping in the shade.

Now write a topic sentence for the supporting details below.

Topic sentence

_____

_____

_____

Supporting details

Many parks have walking trails where people can see plants and wildlife.

Some parks have playgrounds, train rides, and pools to enjoy.

LANGUAGE ARTS

DAY 8 — Photosynthesis

Plants use a process called **photosynthesis** to make sugar. Plants use this sugar as food.

Look at the diagram. Then use the bolded words from the diagram to complete the sentences.

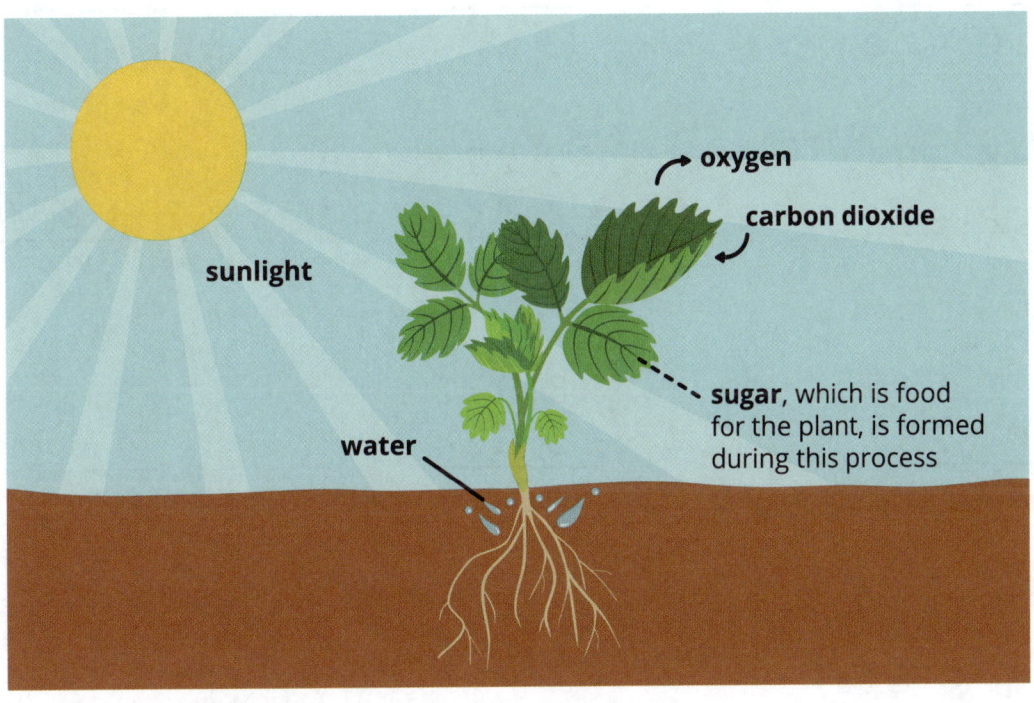

Photosynthesis is a process in which plants use energy from _____ to make their own food. Plants use _____ from the air and _____ from the soil to make _____, which plants use as food. During this process, plants release _____ into the air as a waste product.

DAY 8 — Add and subtract within 10,000

IXL.com skill ID **LPZ**

Add or subtract.

```
    1
  4,017          9,867          1,025
+ 2,456        - 2,315        + 4,364
  -----          -----          -----
  6,473
```

```
  8,364          5,228          2,517
- 5,241        + 2,362        + 3,840
```

```
  5,940          8,972          8,324
+   237        - 5,624        - 1,179
```

Write each missing digit.

```
  3,7□9          7,46□          4,2□1
+ 4,513        - □,820        + 3,650
  -----          -----          -----
  □,242          5,643          7,□31
```

```
  □,41□          5,□14          □,40□
+ 2,□37        -   90□        - 5,□78
  -----          -----          -----
  8,056          □,908          2,024
```

22　MATH

Reading comprehension

Read the passage. Then answer the questions on the next page.

Color-Changing Animals

What do a chameleon, a cuttlefish, and an octopus have in common? They can all quickly change the color of their skin!

While color changing is a pretty awesome skill, these amazing animals actually use it to survive in their environments. Their color-changing abilities allow them to communicate with others of their kind, hide from predators and prey, or control their body temperature.

Chameleons can change color in less than a minute. While many people think chameleons only change color to blend into their surroundings, color changes are also a way to communicate with other chameleons. A bright color can signal that a chameleon is excited, while a dark color can mean it's angry. Chameleons also change color to warm up or cool down.

Cuttlefish are another example of quick color changers. Cuttlefish are ocean animals related to octopuses and squid. Under their skin, cuttlefish have thousands of tiny cells that make color. These cells, called chromatophores, allow cuttlefish to match their surroundings in less than a second. Cuttlefish change color to hunt, hide from predators, and communicate with other cuttlefish.

The fastest color changers of all are octopuses. They also use chromatophore cells to change color in the blink of an eye. Octopuses change color to show their moods and to communicate with other octopuses. They also change color to hide from predators and hunt their prey.

Changing skin color is not just a neat trick for these animals. It's an important part of how they survive in their environments.

DAY 9: Reading comprehension

Use the passage to answer the questions.

What is the main idea of the passage? Put an X next to the correct answer.

_____ Octopuses use special cells to change colors in less than a second.

_____ Some animals can quickly change their skin color to help them survive.

_____ Chameleons change colors to blend into their surroundings.

Which detail does **not** support the main idea? Put an X next to the correct answer.

_____ Chameleons may change colors to warm up or cool down.

_____ Octopuses change color to hide from predators.

_____ Cuttlefish are ocean animals like octopuses and squid.

Based on the passage, what are **three** reasons chameleons, octopuses, and cuttlefish change colors?

1.
2.
3.

Write the correct letter to match each word in the left column with its definition.

_____ communicate   A. an animal that is eaten by other animals

_____ predator   B. to stay alive

_____ prey   C. an animal that eats other animals

_____ survive   D. give information, thoughts, or feelings

DAY 10: Circle challenge

Get creative! Turn each circle into an object, such as a clock or an orange. How many objects can you draw in five minutes?

DAY 10: Scavenger hunt

It's time for a scavenger hunt! Find a different item for each clue. Write the name of each item you find next to the clue.

Clue	
Something made of metal	
Something that shines	
Something with holes	
Something that crunches	
Something made of glass	
Something that is smooth	
Something that rolls	
Something made of wood	
Something that is fluffy	
Something wider than it is tall	
Something that can change shape	
Something that opens and closes	
Something you can see through	
Something that floats in water	
Something heavier than your shoe	

Reading comprehension

Read the first part of the story. Then answer the questions.

The New Librarian

"Are you sure this way is faster?" Rowan asked as he hurried after his sister, Pepper. His library books were due last week, and the library was about to close. If Rowan's books weren't returned today, he would have to pay a fine and face the new librarian, Mr. Silver, tomorrow. And Rowan really didn't want to face an angry dragon.

"You worry too much," Pepper said, rolling her eyes. For a goblin, Pepper sure rolled her eyes a lot.

Rowan didn't like to run because he sometimes tripped on his tail, but he went as fast as he could. He dodged a group of pixies splashing in the puddles from the morning's rain as he chased after Pepper. Suddenly she stopped, and Rowan almost bumped into her. They had reached the library just in time.

Rowan shifted his bag on his shoulder and rushed toward the doors, but his tail got in the way. *Oh no!* Rowan fell, his body twisting as his tail became tangled between his feet. The books tumbled out of the bag, onto the ground...and into a puddle.

Rowan sat on his knees, staring at the books as his eyes filled with tears.

Based on what Pepper says in the second paragraph, which word best describes her? Put an X next to the correct answer.

____ careful   ____ carefree   ____ caring

Reread the last sentence of the passage above. How does Rowan probably feel? Why?

_____

_____

DAY 11 Reading comprehension

Read the next part of the story and answer the questions. Put an X next to the correct answer, or write your answer on the lines.

"It was an accident," said Pepper. She sounded encouraging, but she bit her lip. "Just tell the truth, and he'll understand."

Rowan sighed, his tail drooping to the ground. Mr. Silver would probably never let him borrow books again. Rowan gulped, gathered the wet books, and stood up.

When Rowan and Pepper entered the library, Mr. Silver was sitting at the front desk, polishing his enormous claws.

Too nervous to speak, Rowan simply frowned as he held up the dripping books. But Mr. Silver's red eyes didn't go wide. He didn't even get up from his chair.

"I see," he said. "Bring them here, please."

Rowan placed the books on the desk. Mr. Silver took each one and very carefully blew on the pages. There was no fire, but the heat dried each page in moments.

"No harm done," said Mr. Silver with a smile. "Let me know when you want to borrow more."

Based on the first paragraph above, how does Pepper probably feel?

_____ certain _____ unsure _____ annoyed

How does Rowan probably feel when he enters the library? How do you know?

_____

_____

Which word best describes Mr. Silver?

_____ rude _____ strict _____ understanding

DAY 12 — Add and subtract within 10,000

IXL.com skill ID
83X

Follow the path from start to finish.

START

1,275 → +483 → ☐ → +1,604 → ☐
↓ −851
☐
↓ +4,246
☐ ← +1,951 ← ☐ ← −2,305 ← ☐
↓ −3,880
☐
↓ +7,141
☐ → −5,959 → ☐ → −1,267 → 2,438

FINISH

DAY 12 — Shades of meaning

Read each question and put an X next to the correct answer.

Which is deeper? ____ a lake ____ a pond	Which takes longer to swim across? ____ a river ____ a stream
Which is easier? ____ a hike ____ a walk	Which is smaller? ____ a city ____ a village
Which bite is bigger? ____ a nibble ____ a chomp	Which noise is louder? ____ a shout ____ a whisper
Which would be more painful to touch? ____ a cup of boiling water ____ a cup of hot water	Which is closer to being dry? ____ a soaked towel ____ a damp towel

Draw a picture under each word to show its meaning. Make sure the pictures show how the two words are different!

canoe	ship

30 — LANGUAGE ARTS

DAY 13 Fractions

Show each fraction using the strip model.

$\frac{2}{6}$

$\frac{2}{3}$

$\frac{5}{8}$

Show each fraction on the number line.

$\frac{1}{4}$

0   $\frac{1}{4}$ $\frac{2}{4}$ $\frac{3}{4}$ 1

$\frac{4}{6}$

0   1

$\frac{3}{8}$

0   1

$\frac{1}{3}$

0   1

Become an IXL member for unlimited practice. Get 20% off when you join IXL today! Visit www.ixl.com/workbook/34s for details.

DAY 13: Figurative language

IXL.com skill ID **L7C**

Figurative language is when words are used to mean something different than their usual, everyday meaning.

Find the path from start to finish. Your path should go only through spaces with figurative language.

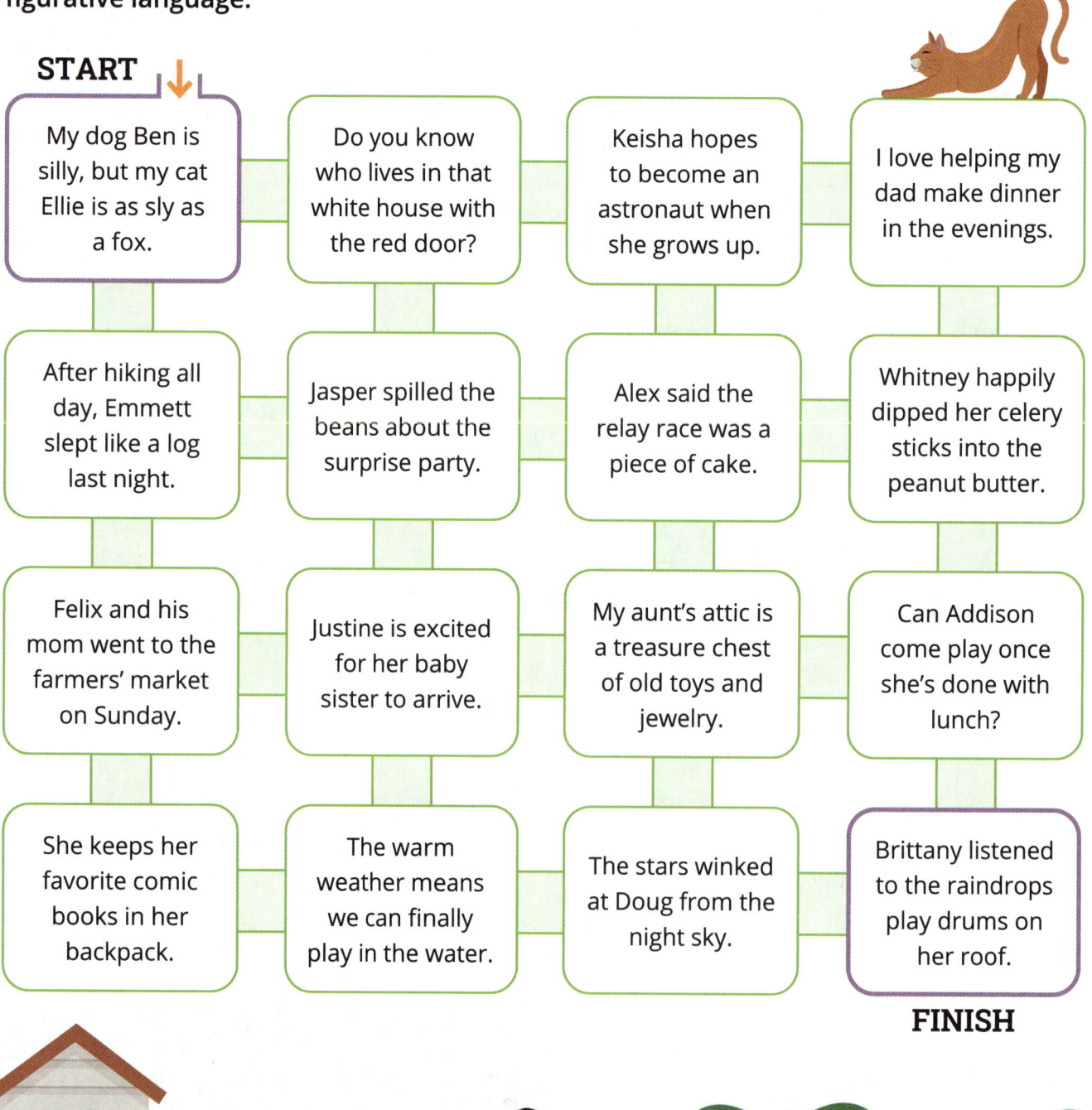

DAY 14: Government

IXL.com skill ID
8HL

There are three levels of government in the United States:

- The **federal** government is in charge of the whole United States.
- A **state** government is in charge of one state.
- A **local** government is in charge of a city, town, or county.

Each space below contains a role or duty of one level of government. Color the spaces using the key.

ORANGE — federal government
BLUE — state government
GREEN — local government

makes laws for the whole United States	builds state highways	meets in the Capitol Building in Washington, D.C.
gives people driver's licenses	is sometimes led by a mayor	prints U.S. dollars
builds playgrounds in a city, town, or county	meets in a state capitol	makes laws for a city, town, or county
is led by the president	is in charge of the United States Armed Forces	is led by a governor
meets at a city hall, town hall, or county seat	makes laws for a state	collects trash from people's houses

 **Brain Break!** Find a partner and create a secret handshake. Use a mix of special movements!

DAY 14: Word problems

The Parkston Polar Bears baseball team is playing against the Bakersville Bulldogs. Answer each question.

The ballpark can hold up to 9,500 fans. If 6,213 fans have already entered the park, how many more fans can join them?

_____ more fans

During the game, 752 hot dogs are sold at the snack bar. Another 1,108 hot dogs are sold in the stands. How many hot dogs are sold during the game in all?

_____ hot dogs

There are 6,258 Polar Bears fans at the game. There are 1,648 Bulldogs fans. How many more fans do the Polar Bears have at the game than the Bulldogs?

_____ more fans

The snack bar starts the day with 7,000 cups. During the game, the snack bar workers give out 6,813 cups. Then they get 2,500 more cups from the storage closet. How many cups does the snack bar have at the end of the game?

_____ cups

Before the game starts, the team store makes $1,095. During the game, the store makes $874. After the game, the store makes $1,563. How much money does the team store make that day?

_____

DAY 15 Sudoku

Complete the sudoku puzzle using the numbers 1–9. Each number must appear only once in each row, column, and block. See the tips at the bottom for help getting started.

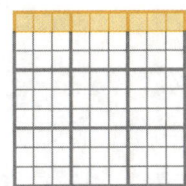
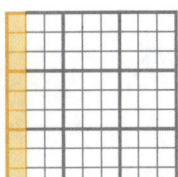
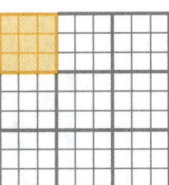

1		2	5	6	8	9	4	
		5	4			3		
	8	9	3		1	2		6
9		8		5	6		3	4
	5	3		1				8
	6	4			7	1	9	
			7					3
3	4	6		2	5	8		
5	9	7		8	3		1	2

Need help getting started?

1. Complete the third column.
2. Complete the bottom left section.
3. Complete the bottom row.
4. Complete the top row.

DAY 15: Multiple-meaning words

IXL.com skill ID **LSF**

Write the multiple-meaning word for each set of definitions. Then use the letters in the circled column to answer the riddle at the bottom of the page.

- a gift
- the time right now

P R E S E N T

- a fenced-in space for an animal
- an ink writing tool

P E N

- the outer part of a tree
- the sound a dog makes

B A R K

- a rubber wheel on a car
- to run out of energy

T I R E

- a kind of water bird
- to bend down quickly

D U C K

- a tool to measure length
- someone who leads

R U L E R

- to jump forward
- the season after winter

S P R I N G

- a metal container
- able to do something

C A N

- the brightness from the sun
- not heavy

L I G H T

What is a star's favorite kind of water? __SPARKLING__

36 © IXL Learning   ENRICHMENT

Weeks 4–6: Overview

Week 4

Math
Multiplication facts
Equivalent fractions

Language arts
Time-order words
Subject-verb agreement
Reading for details

Science
Classifying rocks

Enrichment
Designing a dessert

Week 5

Math
Multiplication word problems
Division facts

Language arts
Subjects and predicates
Transition words
Character point of view

Social studies
State capitals

Enrichment
Logic puzzle
Morse code

Week 6

Math
Multiplication and division
Comparing fractions

Language arts
Comparing two texts
Plural and possessive nouns
Synonyms in context

Science
Magnets

Enrichment
Tongue twisters
Drawing three-dimensional shapes

More ways to learn

Keep the learning going! Use these simple, exciting activities to help you stay active, curious, and creative during your summer break.

See how many activities you can do! Cross off each activity as you complete it.

Learn to juggle. 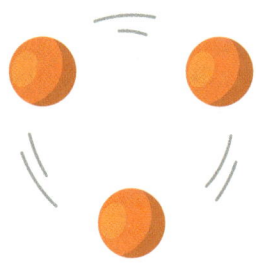	**Write a letter or postcard to someone and send it to them.** 	**Try playing a new sport.** 
Organize something in your room. 	**Play a classic card game like War or Go Fish!** 	**Make up a dance to your favorite song.** 
Construct a fort with blankets and pillows. 	**Make a key chain.** 	**Create your own board game and teach others how to play it.** 

DAY 16 — Multiplication facts

Multiply.

2 × 4 = _____   3 × 8 = _____   7 × 1 = _____

5 × 10 = _____   2 × 6 = _____   0 × 9 = _____

5 × 7 = _____   10 × 7 = _____   5 × 5 = _____

8 × 9 = _____   8 × 0 = _____   6 × 4 = _____

5 × 3 = _____   8 × 6 = _____   9 × 9 = _____

7 × 7 = _____   3 × 9 = _____   4 × 8 = _____

6 × 7 = _____   8 × 8 = _____   9 × 6 = _____

Explore hundreds more topics! Get 20% off when you join IXL today. Scan the QR code or visit www.ixl.com/workbook/34s for details.

DAY 16: Time-order words

Time-order words can make your writing clearer and more interesting. Look at some examples of time-order words below.

Past	recently, earlier, once, yesterday
Present	currently, now, today, tonight
Future	tomorrow, soon, later
Order of events	first, next, then, last, afterward, before, finally

Complete the paragraph with some of the time-order words from the table.

_____Recently_____, high winds from a storm broke the basketball hoop in our neighborhood park. To raise money for a new hoop, a group of us decided to have a yard sale. _____, Dylan and I told our neighbor, Mr. Jordan, that we wanted to use the empty corner lot for the yard sale next Saturday. He thought our idea was great, and he even let us borrow some tables! _____, we need to get the word out to more people. Kayla is making signs _____ to inform our neighbors about the yard sale. _____, she will put the signs up around the neighborhood while the rest of us gather items for the yard sale. With any luck, we will _____ raise enough money to buy a new hoop.

DAY 17: Multiplication facts

Multiply. Draw lines to connect each pair of matching products.

7 × 0 = 0	2 × 9
3 × 6	8 × 7
10 × 4	3 × 10
4 × 4	5 × 8
6 × 5	10 × 2
1 × 9	3 × 3
5 × 4	8 × 2
2 × 2	0 × 5 = 0
7 × 8	2 × 6
3 × 4	4 × 1

Brain Break! Find a sturdy wall or closed door. Press your back against the wall and slide down until it looks like you're sitting in an invisible chair. See how long you can hold this position!

DAY 17: Subject-verb agreement

Underline the subject of each sentence. Then circle the correct verb that goes with each subject.

<u>Laila and Sara</u> (gaze) | gazes   at the stars in the dark night sky.

Asher   practice | **practices**   piano every day.

Our two orange cats   **notice** | notices   the birds on our back porch.

The river in the valley   flow | **flows**   under the old wooden bridge.

The weary travelers   **settle** | settles   into their rooms for the evening.

I   **save** | saves   all of my dad's loose change in a big glass jar.

The bakery down the street   prepare | **prepares**   for the morning rush.

People in the park   **admire** | admires   the amazing chalk artists.

Circle each verb. Then complete the sentence with a subject that correctly matches the verb.

__The train__ (blows) its whistle in three long, loud bursts.

_____ swim laps in the pool every day before breakfast.

_____ smile at the thought of homemade maple pecan ice cream.

_____ leads the kids through the course before the race.

_____ blossom every spring in my uncle's garden.

_____ carves the wood into the shape of an elephant.

DAY 18 Classifying rocks

IXL.com skill ID
75D

There are three main types of rocks:

- **Igneous rocks** are formed when molten rock cools and hardens to form solid rock. They are formed at or below the earth's surface.
- **Sedimentary rocks** are formed when layers of sediment get pressed together to form rock. They are formed below the earth's surface.
- **Metamorphic rocks** are formed when a rock is changed by heating and squeezing. They are formed deep below the earth's surface.

Read the clues about each rock. In the space provided, write whether each rock is igneous, sedimentary, or metamorphic.

Rock A 	**Rock B** 	**Rock C** 
Rock A was formed when layers of sand were pressed together. It is made of tiny grains.	Rock B was formed deep below the earth's surface when rocks were changed by heating and squeezing.	Rock C was formed when molten rock cooled below the earth's surface. It is made of large grains.
sedimentary		

Rock D 	**Rock E** 	**Rock F** 
Rock D was formed when layers of sand, mud, and pebbles pressed together. It is made of grains of different sizes.	Rock E was formed when molten rock cooled at the earth's surface. It has gaps from air and water bubbles.	Rock F was formed when rocks were changed by heating and squeezing. It has dark and light bands.

SCIENCE

Equivalent fractions

Shade in each equivalent fraction. Write the new fraction.

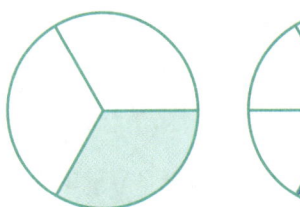 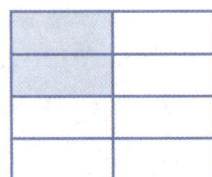

$\frac{1}{3} = \frac{2}{6}$ $\frac{2}{8} =$ _____

 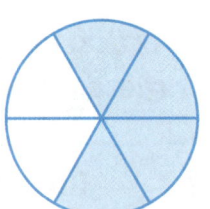

$\frac{1}{2} =$ _____ $\frac{4}{6} =$ _____

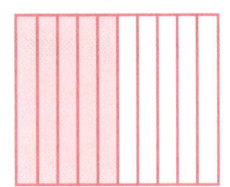 

$\frac{5}{10} =$ _____ $\frac{3}{4} =$ _____

 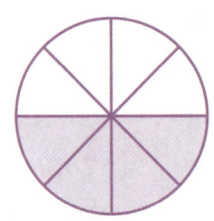

$\frac{2}{2} =$ _____ $\frac{4}{8} =$ _____

DAY 19 Reading comprehension

Read the passage. Then answer the questions on the next page.

Awesome Origami

Have you ever seen the neatly folded paper animals that origami artists make? The art of origami comes from Japan. In origami, you take square sheets of paper and use careful folds to turn the paper into beautiful shapes.

If you want to make origami at home, you first need to gather your tools and materials. The most important material you will need is square paper. You can cut your own or buy special origami paper at a craft store. You also need instructions for the shape you want to make. Do you want to make a fox? A butterfly? Maybe a dragon? You can find step-by-step instructions in books or online.

Once you have gathered your materials, you need to prepare your workspace. You will want a clean, flat surface. This can be a desk, a kitchen table, or even the floor. You might want to use a mat to protect the surface from scratches or glue.

After you have prepared your workspace, you are ready to begin folding. It is important to fold the paper tightly. Many artists fold the paper with their hands first. Then they press down on the fold with a flat tool, such as a ruler. This makes the folds neater and helps the design hold its shape. You must complete all of the folds in the correct order to create the design you want.

Once you complete the project, you can use a bit of glue to make sure the paper holds its shape. See what kinds of fun designs you can make!

While you really only need square paper to do simple origami projects, some artists use special tools to create more **complex** designs. Some tools might include the following:

- Scissors or craft knife
- Metal ruler
- Double-sided tape or glue
- Bone paper folder
- Paper scoring tools
- Self-sealing cutting mat

DAY 19 Reading comprehension

IXL.com skill ID
2TH

Use the passage to answer the questions. Write your answer on the lines, or put an X next to the correct answer.

Where does the art of origami come from? _____

What is the most important material needed to make origami? _____

Why is it helpful to press down on the folds with a flat tool?

_____

_____

What is the purpose of the sidebar in the passage?

____ to give the steps for folding an origami flower

____ to share about the history of origami

____ to tell about special tools used in origami

You can use synonyms and antonyms to help you figure out the meaning of a new word. Which word in the sidebar is an antonym of **complex**?

____ simple   ____ special   ____ scoring

Based on the passage, which of the following is **not** a tool used for origami?

____ a ruler   ____ a stapler   ____ scissors

Try it yourself! Follow the instructions below to fold your own origami fox.

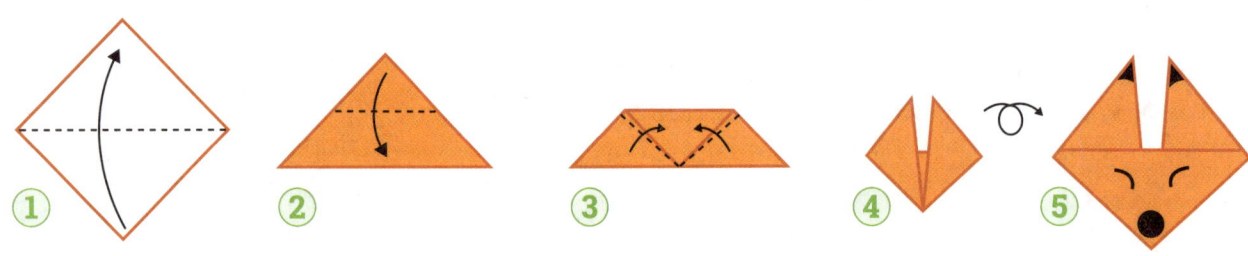

46 © IXL Learning   LANGUAGE ARTS

DAY 20: Dessert challenge

The Daring Dessert Company wants you to design their next summer treat—a brand-new frozen dessert! Your frozen invention might have bold new flavors, interesting textures, or unusual ingredients. You might even create a completely new type of frozen treat!

The new dessert must include the following:
- at least two flavors
- at least three ingredients
- something that makes it different from other desserts
- a catchy name

Use the space below to brainstorm ideas for your new frozen treat.

What will your dessert be?
What flavors will it include?
What ingredients will be used?
What makes this dessert different from other frozen desserts?
List some ideas for a catchy name for this dessert.

DAY 20: Dessert challenge

Now you need to design a poster to show off your frozen treat! The poster should include the following:

- the name of the dessert
- a full-color drawing of the treat
- labels to point out important details

Use the space below to design your poster. Under the drawing, write a short paragraph to persuade people to try the new frozen dessert.

DAY 21: Subjects and predicates

Every sentence has a complete subject and a complete predicate. The **complete subject** tells who or what is doing something. The **complete predicate** tells what the subject is doing. Look at the example below.

<u>Her best friend</u> <u>jumps in the pool</u>.

Read each sentence below. Underline the complete subject in blue. Underline the complete predicate in orange.

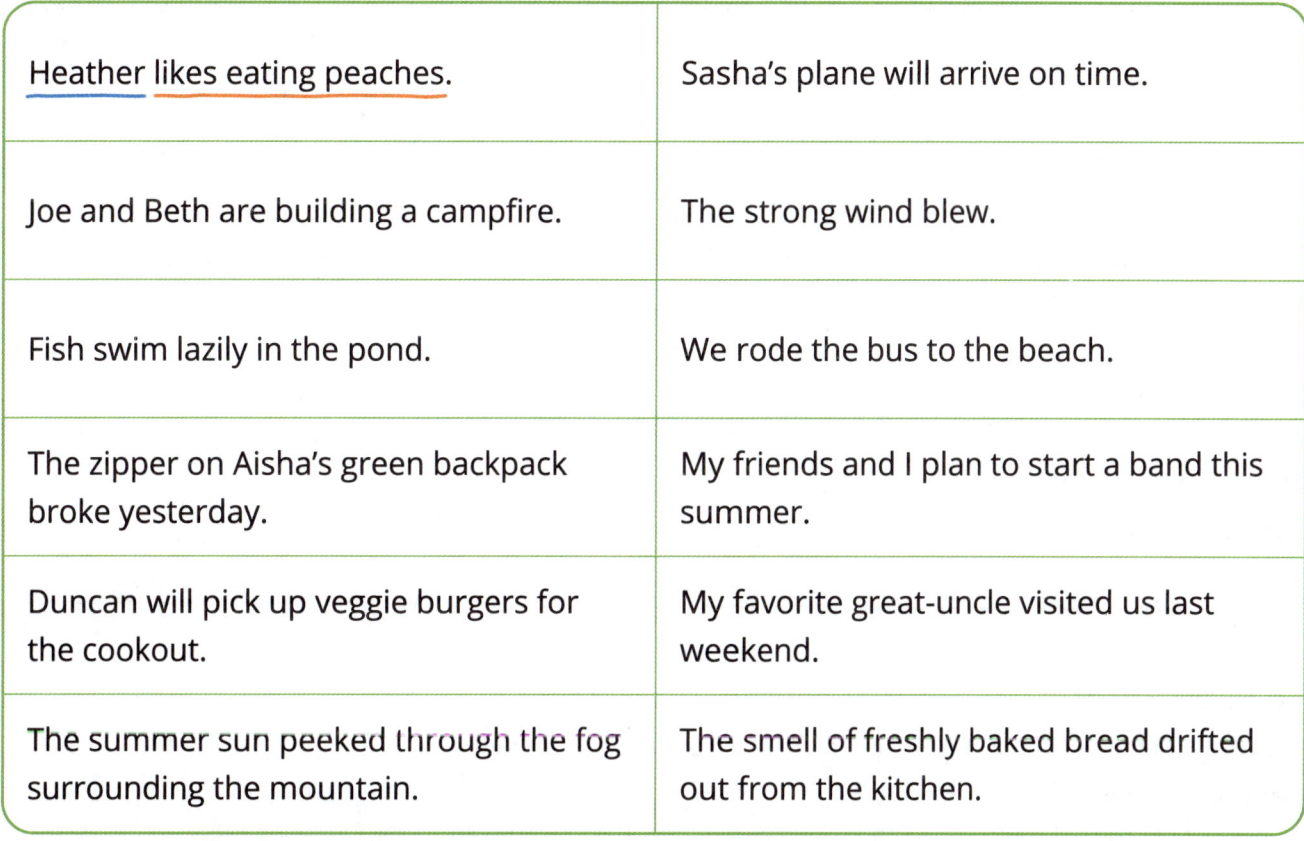

<u>Heather</u> <u>likes eating peaches.</u>	Sasha's plane will arrive on time.
Joe and Beth are building a campfire.	The strong wind blew.
Fish swim lazily in the pond.	We rode the bus to the beach.
The zipper on Aisha's green backpack broke yesterday.	My friends and I plan to start a band this summer.
Duncan will pick up veggie burgers for the cookout.	My favorite great-uncle visited us last weekend.
The summer sun peeked through the fog surrounding the mountain.	The smell of freshly baked bread drifted out from the kitchen.

Write two complete sentences. Underline the complete subject in blue and the complete predicate in orange.

1.

2.

DAY 21 — Word problems

Answer each question.

Emir writes 5 thank-you cards. He puts 3 stickers on each card. How many stickers does Emir use altogether?

_____ stickers

Mrs. Patel bakes 4 pizzas for a pizza party. She cuts each pizza into 8 pieces. How many pieces of pizza are there in all?

_____ pieces of pizza

Chris works at Fresh Blooms flower shop. He puts lilies into 7 different vases. He puts 6 lilies in each vase. How many lilies does he use altogether?

_____ lilies

There are 6 tables at Mirella's Cafe. Each table has 4 seats. How many seats are there in all?

_____ seats

Coach Sanchez sets up 7 rows of cones at soccer practice. He puts 9 cones in each row. How many cones does Coach Sanchez use in all?

_____ cones

DAY 22: Transition words

IXL.com skill ID
5HN

Transition words and phrases can help readers understand how two ideas are related. Look at some examples below.

Purpose	Transitions
Show the order of events in time	first, next, afterward, earlier, finally, later
Show cause and effect	as a result, for this reason, therefore
Add a new example or idea	for instance, for example, also, additionally

Complete each sentence with a transition word or phrase from the table.

A new tea shop just opened down the street. __Additionally__, a game store will be opening this summer.

Our team's end-of-season celebration will begin with dinner. _____, we will head to the awards ceremony to receive our trophies.

For weeks, I forgot to water my plants. _____, they dried up and lost their leaves.

We bought a rainbow of vegetables at the farmers' market. _____, we got red tomatoes, yellow squash, and purple carrots.

This morning, Dad noticed that the car needed gas. _____, we had to stop at the gas station on the way to softball practice.

Sasha spent three long months on her coding project. _____, she's ready to present her work to the robotics team.

I'm thinking about starting a book club. _____, I need to make a list of all the people who might be interested in joining.

Day 22: Division facts

IXL.com skill ID **M8T**

Divide.

9 ÷ 3 = _____

10 ÷ 2 = _____

24 ÷ 4 = _____

35 ÷ 7 = _____

14 ÷ 7 = _____

64 ÷ 8 = _____

20 ÷ 5 = _____

90 ÷ 9 = _____

18 ÷ 2 = _____

49 ÷ 7 = _____

63 ÷ 9 = _____

36 ÷ 9 = _____

32 ÷ 4 = _____

48 ÷ 8 = _____

45 ÷ 5 = _____

60 ÷ 10 = _____

42 ÷ 6 = _____

80 ÷ 8 = _____

56 ÷ 8 = _____

28 ÷ 7 = _____

72 ÷ 9 = _____

Boost your learning and save 20%. Join IXL today! Scan the QR code or visit www.ixl.com/workbook/34s for details.

Reading comprehension

Read the story. Then answer the questions on the next page.

An Amazing Adventure

I had just placed the last sack of beans on top of the pile behind the counter when Mama called out to me. "Lucy, a customer!" she said, pointing toward the front door. I looked over and saw a boy staring at the floor, nervously twisting his hat in his hands.

Early spring has always been my favorite time of year. That's when our family's supply store gets really busy as folks get ready to head out West on the Oregon Trail. Some go for the good farmland out there, others hope for a better life, and a few just want an adventure. I love listening to the travelers' stories, especially other kids', and imagining what my own adventures might be like.

"Are you all set for your long journey?" I asked the boy as I approached him.

"My family is, but I don't know if I want to leave everything behind," he said, poking a rock on the floor with the toe of his boot. "Or every*one*."

I nodded. I've met lots of kids who feel unsure about leaving. I said, "The trail guides will show you some beautiful sights you'll never forget."

The boy sighed. "That's what my pa says. But what if it's scary or I get lonely?"

I answered gently, "You won't be alone, though. Hundreds of folks will be traveling together. Your new best friend might be just down the road!"

The boy looked at me, his eyes lighting up. "I didn't think of it that way before."

"And they say we find our courage on the journey," I added. "My family is heading out next month. I can't wait!"

The boy smiled. "Maybe we'll see each other on the trail then. I'm Henry," he said.

"Pleased to meet you, Henry. I'm Lucy. It sure will be one amazing adventure!"

DAY 23 Reading comprehension

IXL.com skill ID
N7R

Use the story to answer the questions.

What is the setting of the story? Put an X next to the correct answer.

_____ a family farm in the West   _____ a supply store near the Oregon Trail

_____ a boy's hat shop   _____ a restaurant in Oregon

Why is early spring Lucy's favorite time of year?

_____

_____

Think about how Lucy and Henry each feel about the Oregon Trail at the beginning of the story. How are their points of view different? How do you know? Complete the table.

	Point of view	Evidence
Lucy		
Henry		

Circle **three** words that best describe Lucy.

curious   fearful   shy   adventurous   friendly

How does the conversation with Lucy impact Henry?

_____

_____

54 © IXL Learning   LANGUAGE ARTS

DAY 24 Equivalent fractions

Label the missing fractions on each blank number line. Then write the equivalent fraction.

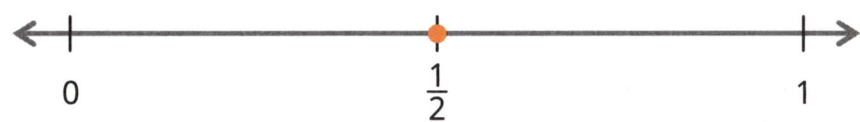

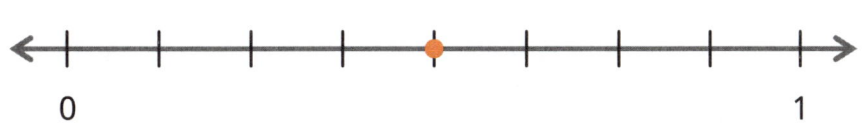

$\dfrac{1}{2} = \dfrac{\square}{\square}$

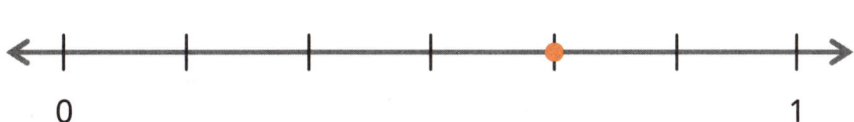

$\dfrac{2}{3} = \dfrac{\square}{\square}$

Fill in each blank.

$\dfrac{1}{2} = \dfrac{\square}{4}$ $\dfrac{2}{4} = \dfrac{\square}{8}$ $\dfrac{1}{2} = \dfrac{\square}{6}$

$\dfrac{1}{3} = \dfrac{\square}{6}$ $\dfrac{1}{2} = \dfrac{\square}{10}$ $\dfrac{3}{4} = \dfrac{\square}{8}$

Brain Break! Take ten baby steps. Then take ten giant steps. Now, try walking on your heels or on your toes. Can you go backwards?

DAY 24 State capitals

For each capital city, write the name of its state. You can use a map to help.

Alaska	Maine	New Jersey	Washington
Arizona	Michigan	North Carolina	West Virginia
Illinois	Montana	~~Rhode Island~~	Wisconsin
Kentucky	Nebraska	Texas	Wyoming

Providence   _Rhode Island_   Austin   _____

Phoenix   _____   Olympia   _____

Madison   _____   Augusta   _____

Frankfort   _____   Raleigh   _____

Cheyenne   _____   Springfield   _____

Trenton   _____   Helena   _____

Charleston   _____   Juneau   _____

Lansing   _____   Lincoln   _____

DAY 25 Logic puzzle

IXL.com skill ID
YWU

Elena is performing in her town's talent show! Use the information in the table and the clues below to write the order of performers.

Performer	Talent	Length of act
Elena	drum solo	2 minutes 30 seconds
Carlos	magic show	4 minutes 15 seconds
Liam	martial arts	2 minutes 45 seconds
Jin	singing	3 minutes 15 seconds
Gabe	guitar solo	3 minutes
Kiara	dance	4 minutes 5 seconds
Olivia	piano solo	3 minutes 45 seconds
Lucas	juggling	2 minutes
Mila	comedy	3 minutes 55 seconds

Clues:

- The longest act is last.
- The person with the shortest name performs first.
- The fourth performer's name and talent start with the same letter.
- The drum solo is the eighth act.
- The shortest act is after the guitar solo.
- The second act lasts more than 4 minutes.
- The sixth act is 10 seconds longer than the seventh act.

Order of performers

1.
2.
3.
4.
5.
6.
7.
8.
9.

ENRICHMENT

DAY 25 Morse code

Morse code is a special way of communicating using a series of dots and dashes to represent letters and numbers. Before phones and the internet, people used telegraphs to send messages in Morse code over long distances.

Morse Code Alphabet

A ·—	B —···	C —·—·	D —··	E ·	F ··—·	G ——·	H ····	I ··
J ·———	K —·—	L ·—··	M ——	N —·	O ———	P ·——·	Q ——·—	R ·—·
S ···	T —	U ··—	V ···—	W ·——	X —··—	Y —·——	Z ——··	

Below are some nicknames for planets in our solar system. Use the key above to decode the name of each planet.

Nickname	Planet name
The Red Planet	—· · ·—· ··· (MARS)
The Blue Planet	· ·— ·—· — ···· (EARTH)
The Ringed Planet	··· ·— — ·· ·—· —· (SATURN)
The Swift Planet	—· · ·—· —·· ··— ·—· —·—— (MERCURY)

Try it! Write your name in Morse code below.

_____

58 © IXL Learning   ENRICHMENT

DAILY NEWS

Grand Opening of Skate Park

Yesterday was the grand opening of Greenville's Southside Skate Park. Skaters of all ages came out, eager to explore the new space. With colorful designs painted throughout, the park was a sight to see!

Skaters wasted no time in trying out the new ramps, rails, and half-pipes. Some even formed teams for friendly skateboarding contests.

Families and friends gathered around, enjoying the fun and cheering on the skaters. Some of the younger visitors danced to music played by DJ Disco Flip. The weather was perfect, and food trucks served hot dogs, burgers, and frozen lemonade to the crowd.

College students from the nearby skateboarding school were also there showing off their skills and offering free skateboarding lessons. Their moves wowed visitors, like Emily, age 8. "I loved seeing them do slides and **kickflips**. It was so cool!" she said.

Southside Skate Park will be open every day from 9 A.M. to 8 P.M. You can visit the park's website to learn more about rules, events, and contests.

Which of the following details was **not** included in the article?

____ what the place looked like

____ who went to the event

____ what time the event happened

____ what food was served

Based on the text, what is a **kickflip**?

____ a type of skateboard

____ a skateboarding trick

____ a new dance move

____ the name of a food truck

DAY 26 Reading comprehension

Read the letter. Then complete the table using information from both passages about the grand opening of the skate park.

Dear Chris,

I went with some friends from my neighborhood to the grand opening of the new skate park yesterday. It was even more awesome than I thought it would be!

We spent the whole day there skating and cheering each other on. There were tons of rails and ramps, and even two half-pipes to try out. We even met some other neighborhood kids who like to skate, and we traded skateboarding tips with them.

One of the best parts was that some older kids from the skateboarding school down the road were there giving free lessons and showing us new tricks. They gave me some tips to help improve my ollie!

Oh, and guess what? The mayor gave away a prize to one person who went to the event, and I won! I got a cool new helmet with black and green stripes.

I can't wait for you to visit so we can check out the new skate park together!

Talk to you soon,
Troy

Complete the table with two details in each section.

Details ONLY in the newspaper article	Details ONLY in Troy's letter
•	•
•	•

Details in both
•
•

DAY 27: Multiply and divide

IXL.com skill ID **WQT**

Complete the puzzle.

Day 27: Magnets

Every magnet has two poles, or ends. A magnet's **north pole** is often marked **N**, and a magnet's **south pole** is often marked **S**. Two magnets can push or pull each other without touching, based on the position of their poles.

When different poles are close to each other, the magnets pull together, or **attract**.

When the same poles are close to each other, the magnets push apart, or **repel**.

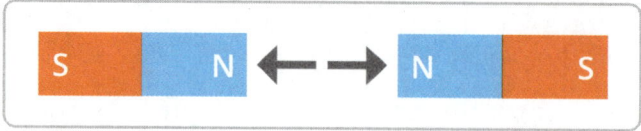

Each picture shows magnets that would attract or repel. Circle the correct answer.

S N S N attract repel	N S S N attract repel
 S N S N attract repel	S N S N attract repel
 S N N S attract repel	 N S (horseshoe) S N (diamond) attract repel

DAY 28: Plural and possessive nouns

Find the plural or possessive error in each sentence. Cross out the error and write the correction above it.

Tracy's
~~Tracys'~~ dream is to have her own horses someday.

Mr. Nakamura's windows' need to be cleaned.

The rockets engines lifted the spacecraft into the air.

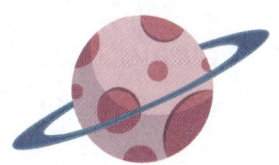

Yolanda's family rode their bikes' on the path by the river.

Last summer, my cities gardens were bursting with color.

The childrens library held many special events this month.

As he neared the top of the trail, Pedros' legs started getting tired.

Jessie's mountain of book's tumbled out of her arms.

Both baker's cakes made it through the first round of the contest.

The girls eyes opened wide when they saw the giant statues.

The farmer's rabbit's smelled the fresh hay before they saw it.

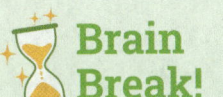 **Brain Break!** Check in with your five senses. Name five things you can see, four things you can hear, three things you can feel, two things you can smell, and one thing you can taste.

Day 28: Word problems

Mateo is opening a lemonade stand! Answer each question.

Mateo uses 7 lemons to make each batch of lemonade. How many lemons does he need to make 4 batches?

_____ lemons

Mateo buys 72 plastic cups. The cups are sold in packs of 8. How many packs does he buy?

_____ packs

Mateo buys 8 packs of little umbrellas to decorate the cups. Each pack has 10 umbrellas. How many umbrellas does Mateo buy?

_____ umbrellas

Mateo uses 20 cups of water to make 4 batches of lemonade. How many cups of water does he use for each batch?

_____ cups of water

Mateo sells 9 cups of lemonade in the first hour his stand is open! He charges $3 for each cup of lemonade. How much money does he make in the first hour?

_____

DAY 29: Synonyms in context

IXL.com skill ID
WZZ

Each set of sentences contains a pair of synonyms. Circle the synonym of the word in bold.

Grandpa and his (buddy) John get breakfast every week. John has been Grandpa's closest **companion** for fifty years.	I followed a sweet **aroma** into the kitchen. I simply can't walk away from the scent of baking cookies.
On a hot day, a spot in the shade is **ideal** for a picnic. The patch of grass under those leafy trees is perfect!	Let's go for a **brisk** walk down the beach to get some exercise before dinner. Try to keep up with my quick pace!
We had a calm morning at the library. After an hour of **serene** reading time, we went to lunch.	The movie was confusing to me! I found the many twists and turns in the story **perplexing**.

Draw lines to match each bold word with its definition. Use the synonyms from the sentences above to help you.

companion	a pleasant smell
ideal	hard to understand
serene	a friend
aroma	quiet and peaceful
brisk	lively, active, or fast
perplexing	the best

(companion — a friend)

Get 20% off when you join IXL today! Scan the QR code for details.

DAY 29 Compare fractions

Use the number lines to compare each pair of fractions using > or < .

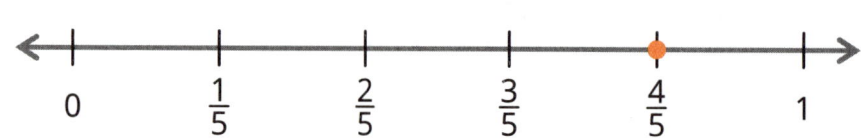

$\frac{2}{5} \bigcirc \frac{4}{5}$

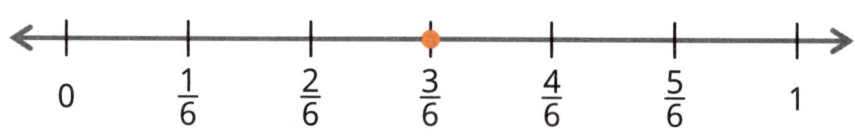

$\frac{3}{6} \bigcirc \frac{3}{8}$

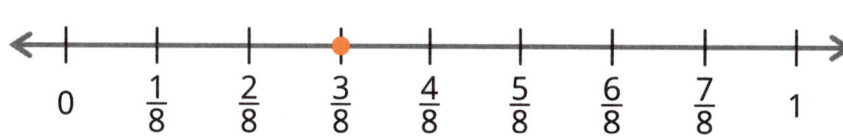

Compare each pair of fractions using > or < .

$\frac{3}{4} \bigcirc \frac{1}{4}$ $\frac{1}{8} \bigcirc \frac{1}{2}$ $\frac{1}{3} \bigcirc \frac{2}{3}$

$\frac{6}{10} \bigcirc \frac{6}{8}$ $\frac{4}{6} \bigcirc \frac{5}{6}$ $\frac{6}{8} \bigcirc \frac{5}{8}$

$\frac{9}{10} \bigcirc \frac{7}{10}$ $\frac{4}{5} \bigcirc \frac{4}{6}$ $\frac{2}{5} \bigcirc \frac{2}{4}$

DAY 30: Tongue twisters

A **tongue twister** is a group of words that is difficult to say because it has many similar sounds. Tongue twisters usually repeat the same sound or go back and forth between two sounds. This can make it feel like your tongue is twisted up!

Try saying these two popular tongue twisters out loud. Notice the repeated sounds.

Peter Piper picked a peck of pickled peppers.

She sells seashells by the seashore.

Create a tongue twister using each sound provided below.

J	
B	
Th	

Now, choose any sound you like and create your own tongue twister.

ENRICHMENT

DAY 30: Draw three-dimensional shapes

Look at the steps below explaining how to draw three-dimensional shapes.

1 Draw a two-dimensional shape. Shapes with straight sides are easier than those with curves.

2 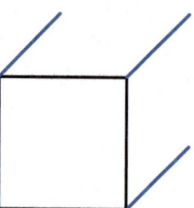 Draw diagonal lines extending from all but one of the corners. The lines should be parallel.

3 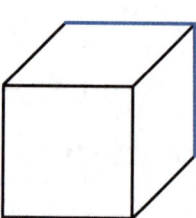 Connect the parallel lines. Make sure these lines are parallel with the original shape.

Turn the two-dimensional shapes below into three-dimensional shapes. Follow steps two and three above.

Weeks 7–9: Overview

Week 7

Math
Multiplication patterns
Multiplying by multiples of 10

Language arts
Irregular past tense
Homophones
Theme

Social studies
Types of resources

Enrichment
Fill-in-the-blank story

Week 8

Math
Rounding numbers
Area

Language arts
Opinion statements
Identifying causes and effects
Complete sentences

Science
Animal adaptations

Enrichment
Analogies
Name art

Week 9

Math
Area of compound shapes
Multiplying using grids

Language arts
Rhyme scheme
Pronouns
Opinion writing

Social studies
Landmarks and monuments

Enrichment
Riddles
Logic puzzle

More ways to learn

Keep the learning going! Use these simple, exciting activities to help you stay active, curious, and creative during your summer break.

See how many activities you can do! Cross off each activity as you complete it.

Plan your dream vacation. 	Help someone with a household task. 	Turn your recyclables into something new and useful. 
Hold a fashion show with clothes from your closet. 	Take a notebook outside and create a nature journal. 	Make homemade ice pops. 
Learn to draw a character you love. 	Play charades with friends or family. 	Create an exercise plan with squats, push-ups, and jumping jacks. 

DAY 31: Multiplication patterns

Multiply. Notice the pattern in each set of equations.

6 × 3 = __18__
6 × 30 = __180__
6 × 300 = __1,800__

4 × 8 = _____
4 × 80 = _____
4 × 800 = _____

7 × 2 = _____
7 × 20 = _____
7 × 200 = _____

8 × 6 = _____
8 × 60 = _____
8 × 600 = _____

3 × 5 = _____
3 × 50 = _____
3 × 500 = _____

9 × 4 = _____
9 × 40 = _____
9 × 400 = _____

3 × 7 = _____
3 × 70 = _____
3 × 700 = _____

5 × 2 = _____
5 × 20 = _____
5 × 200 = _____

6 × 5 = _____
6 × 50 = _____
6 × 500 = _____

Multiply.

8 × 70 = _____
2 × 80 = _____
7 × 600 = _____

4 × 400 = _____
9 × 500 = _____
5 × 80 = _____

3 × 90 = _____
8 × 900 = _____
6 × 600 = _____

DAY 31 — Irregular past tense

Fill in the blanks. Write the past-tense form of each verb.

The campers __began__ gathering wood for the campfire.
(begin)

Last summer, Ziggy _____ swim lessons at the pool.
(teach)

What happened when you _____ your first tooth?
(lose)

The neighbors _____ a treehouse for their kids.
(build)

We _____ to Grandpa on the phone last week.
(speak)

Who _____ the menu for this year's picnic?
(choose)

Ellie _____ the book was better than the movie.
(think)

Last August, we _____ nine hours to visit my Aunt Jeanie.
(drive)

I can't believe I _____ to take pictures of the amazing view!
(forget)

The sky _____ dark with clouds just before the rain started.
(become)

Surprisingly, Hadley's little brother _____ the bow tie all night long.
(wear)

Wes and Garrett _____ at the airport before their flight to Atlanta.
(meet)

DAY 32 — Multiply by multiples of 10

IXL.com skill ID **2RP**

Find the path from start to finish. Move in the direction of the correct answers until you reach the end.

START ↓

4 × 60	240	8 × 200	160	3 × 90
2,400		1,600		270
5 × 800	400	9 × 40	360	7 × 600
4,000		36		4,200
7 × 80	120	4 × 300	140	2 × 70
560		1,200		1,400
9 × 60	5,400	6 × 50	300	8 × 90
540		3,000		720
8 × 50	400	7 × 400	2,800	**FINISH**

Brain Break! Take a deep belly breath and hold it for three counts. Laugh as you release the breath. Do this five times or until it becomes a real laugh!

DAY 32 Resources

IXL.com skill ID
VSX

There are three main types of resources:

- **Human resources** are people who produce a good or service.
- **Natural resources** are useful things that come directly from nature.
- **Capital resources** are tools that help people produce goods or services.

Write each resource from the word bank under the correct category. Then write one more example of each resource type at the bottom of each column.

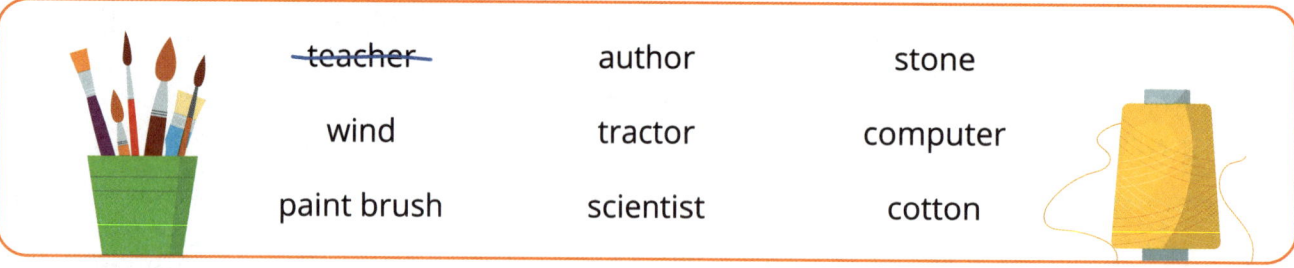

Human resources	Natural resources	Capital resources
• teacher	•	•
•	•	•
•	•	•
•	•	•

Many goods require all three types of resources. Look at the resources needed to make a wooden table. Think of another good and list the resources needed to make it.

Good	Human resources	Natural resources	Capital resources
wooden table	carpenter	wood	hammer, nails

DAY 33 Homophones

IXL.com skill ID **VNC**

Homophones are words that sound alike but are spelled differently and have different meanings.

Circle the correct homophone in each sentence below.

The   deer | dear   jumped over the fence and ran across the meadow.

After lunch, I   road | rode   my bike to the park.

The purple   flour | flower   from your garden smells delightful.

I looked under the bed but still didn't   fined | find   my missing sock.

Abby and Devin   threw | through   a surprise party for their dad's birthday.

The cat stretched out on the bed and licked   its | it's   front paw.

Sal wants to   write | right   a letter to his cousins in Alaska.

Don't forget that   your | you're   riding home with Aunt Jackie tomorrow.

Grandpa read   allowed | aloud   to us from an old storybook.

We watched the beautiful   seen | scene   taking place in the town square.

The speed boat created waves as it   passed | past   us on the lake.

Write a sentence with each of the three homophones below.

sent	
cent	
scent	

DAY 33 — Compare fractions

Plot the fractions on the number lines. Then compare each pair of fractions using >, <, or = .

 $\frac{3}{4} \bigcirc \frac{7}{8}$

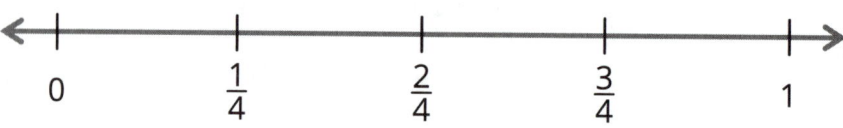

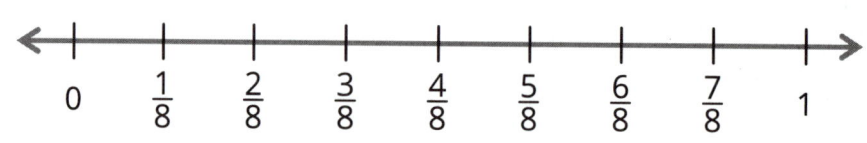

 $\frac{4}{6} \bigcirc \frac{2}{3}$

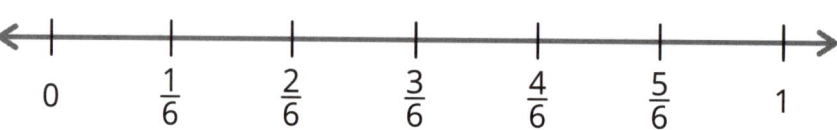

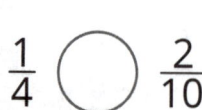 $\frac{1}{4} \bigcirc \frac{2}{10}$

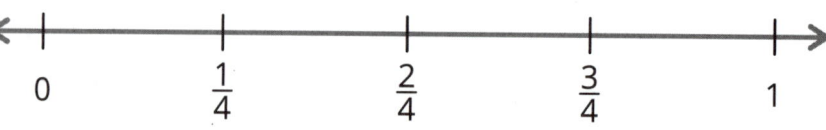

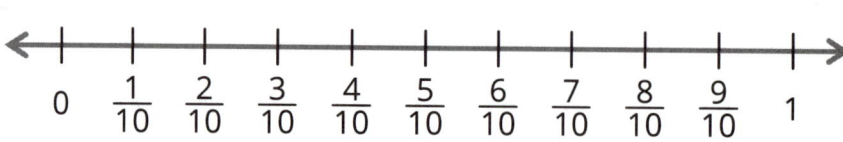

Dive into more practice with IXL! Get 20% off when you join IXL today.

Scan this QR code for details.

Reading comprehension

Read the fable. Then answer the questions on the next page.

The Daring Climb

Elsie watched with wonder as the other mountain goats leaped up the tall cliff with ease. Only the most skilled climbers could reach the grassy peak, dotted with the sweetest wildflowers. Elsie longed to taste summer's first blooms and look out over the whole valley.

One day, Elsie decided she was ready to climb the cliff herself. "I want to try climbing, too," Elsie said to her older cousin Miriam.

With gentle kindness, Miriam showed Elsie how to balance on the steep slopes and place each hoof carefully on the best rocks. They practiced each day, and Elsie gradually climbed farther up the cliff.

After a few days, Elsie felt ready to do the whole climb and taste her reward. She started out strong and sure. *This is easy!* she thought. But about halfway up the cliff, a rock came loose beneath her back hoof. Elsie lost her balance and slid all the way down in a tumble of hooves and dust. She frowned, shaking the dust from her fur.

"You're getting better each time you try," Miriam encouraged her. "These mistakes are an important part of learning." Elsie was frustrated, but she wasn't ready to give up yet.

The next day, Elsie tried again. She paid attention to every step, testing each stone before putting her full weight on it. She avoided rushing, took breaks to catch her breath, and stopped on small ledges to rest her tired legs. Higher and higher she climbed, remembering each lesson Miriam had taught her.

At last, Elsie's hooves touched the sweet-smelling grass at the top. The other goats bleated their cheers. Elsie proudly feasted on the wildflowers, taking in the amazing views of the valley from her hard-won **perch**.

DAY 34 Reading comprehension

IXL.com skill ID
7T9

Use the fable to answer the questions. Put an X next to the correct answer, or write your answer on the lines.

How does Miriam help Elsie prepare for her climb?

_____ She tells her to climb alone and not be scared.

_____ She shows her the best path to take up the cliff.

_____ She teaches her how to balance and choose the best rocks.

How does Elsie feel after her fall? How do you know? Give evidence from the story to support your answer.

_____

_____

What are **three** things Elsie does differently after her fall?

1.	
2.	
3.	

Put a ☐box☐ around **two** words that describe Elsie. ⓒircle **two** words that describe Miriam.

    brave   helpful   daring   silly   wise   selfish

What is the main theme or lesson of the fable?

_____ Learning from your mistakes can lead to success.

_____ Never try anything too difficult.

_____ Always ask for help when things get hard.

What is the meaning of **perch** as it is used in the story?

_____ type of flower   _____ high resting spot   _____ life lesson

LANGUAGE ARTS

DAY 35: Fill-in-the-blank story

Complete the chart with words that match the details in the left column. Then use your words to make a silly story on the next page.

Name 1	
Name 2	
Town name	
Noun 1 (plural)	
Noun 2 (plural)	
Fruit	
Animal 1	
Past-tense verb	
Food (plural)	
Animal 2 (plural)	
Adjective	
Present-tense verb	
Number greater than 1	
Unit of time (plural)	

DAY 35 Fill-in-the-blank story

Fill in the blanks with the words you chose on the previous page. Remember to use correct capitalization in your story. Then read your silly story out loud!

_____ and _____ arrived at the _____
    name 1   name 2   town name

Art Museum. Inside, the friends grabbed a map to decide where to go first.

"Ooh, I want to see the _____ in the west wing," said
                                    noun 1 (plural)

_____. There, they saw lots of paintings hanging on the walls.
    name 1

_____ was amazed at one called *A Thousand* _____.
    name 2   noun 2 (plural)

Next, they went to see the art located outside. _____ took a picture
                                                                name 1

in front of a piece called *The* _____ *and the* _____.
                                          fruit   animal 1

Just then _____'s stomach _____. "I guess that
                    name 1   past-tense verb

_____ is making me hungry!"
    fruit

The two friends went to the café and ordered _____. They ate their
                                                                   food (plural)

food like a couple of hungry _____.
                                    animal 2 (plural)

After their _____ meal, the friends were ready to see more.
                    adjective

They both agreed that they could _____ for _____
                                            present-tense verb   number greater than 1

more _____.
       unit of time (plural)

ENRICHMENT

DAY 36 Opinion statements

IXL.com skill ID
GC2

Read each paragraph below. Underline the sentence in each paragraph where the writer states an opinion.

Did you know that when you sleep, your brain is actually quite active? <u>Sleep is the most important thing you can do for your brain.</u> Scientists say our brains need a chance to rest and recharge, just like our bodies do.

The ukulele is the easiest instrument to learn how to play. It is smaller than a guitar and has four strings instead of six. Many children learn to play ukulele. Most people can learn to play a full song in a day!

Historical fiction is a type of writing that is part history and part fiction. Some of the story details are facts from the past, while other parts are made up. These stories can help people learn about the past. Everyone should read historical fiction.

The aquarium in my town has giant tanks filled with colorful fish. They even have sharks that swim right in front of you! There is also a touch tank where you can touch starfish and horseshoe crabs. Every time I go, I learn something new. The aquarium is such an interesting place to visit!

Read the paragraph below. Write an opinion statement based on the author's other sentences.

My bunny, Marlow, rings a bell to get a treat. He hops over to me when I call his name. He can even jump through hoops!

Opinion: _____

_____

Brain Break! Using your finger, trace your name once on a smooth surface, once on a rough surface, and once on a soft surface. Notice how different each surface feels.

DAY 36 Rounding numbers

Round each number to the nearest ten.

48 __50__   73 _____   25 _____

56 _____   234 _____   197 _____

585 _____   743 _____   4,846 _____

3,718 _____   1,922 _____   9,265 _____

Round each number to the nearest hundred.

713 __700__   852 _____   435 _____

267 _____   384 _____   648 _____

994 _____   2,650 _____   4,329 _____

1,171 _____   5,525 _____   8,153 _____

Boost your learning and save 20%. Join IXL today! Scan the QR code or visit www.ixl.com/workbook/34s for details.

Reading comprehension

Read the passage below. Then answer the questions on the next page.

Great Smoky Mountains National Park

Do you dream of seeing ancient mountains, tall trees, and amazing animals all in one place? Then visit Great Smoky Mountains National Park! This beautiful park is on the border between Tennessee and North Carolina. It's located in a mountain range known as "the Smokies," which gets its name from the light mist and fog hanging over the mountains.

All that water in the air from the mist and fog helps keep the plants and trees healthy and green. Tall trees, such as pine, oak, and hickory, grow well here and form a thick forest. Visitors come from all over to see the beauty of the park's mountainous forests and tumbling waterfalls.

The forest is home to many animals, including black bears, deer, and salamanders. The park is even known as the "Salamander Capital of the World" because so many different types of salamanders live there. These amphibians love the park's cool, damp forests and clear mountain streams. The park is also one of the few places in North America where you can find synchronous fireflies. These fireflies are special because they all light up at the same time!

The many different plants and animals in the park depend on each other. Trees provide homes and food for countless animals, from tiny insects to larger mammals. The clear mountain streams, fed by the misty air, are important for fish and amphibians. This balance between land, water, and wildlife makes the Smokies a special place for nature lovers.

Great Smoky Mountains National Park is truly a wonderful place to visit. Plan a trip with your family, and enjoy the natural beauty of the Great Smoky Mountains!

DAY 37 Reading comprehension

Use the passage to answer the questions. Write your answers in the spaces provided.

Where is Great Smoky Mountains National Park?

_____

Complete the table with causes and effects from the passage.

Cause	Effect
	The mountains got the name "smoky."
There is a lot of water in the air.	
	The park is known as the "Salamander Capital of the World."

List **two** reasons that the Great Smoky Mountains are an ideal home for salamanders.

1.
2.

What is the author's opinion of Great Smoky Mountains National Park? Give evidence from the passage to support your answer.

_____

_____

_____

DAY 38 — Estimate products

Estimate each product. Round the two-digit factor to the nearest ten, and then multiply.

There are 18 tables in Pronto Pizza. There are 4 chairs at each table. About how many chairs are there in Pronto Pizza?

__18__ × __4__ is about __20__ × __4__ = __80__ chairs

There are 36 fruit chews in a package of Flora Zest Fruit Chews. About how many fruit chews are in 3 packages?

_____ × _____ is about _____ × _____ = _____ fruit chews

Amari bakes 7 batches of mini muffins. Each batch has 24 muffins. About how many mini muffins does Amari bake?

_____ × _____ is about _____ × _____ = _____ mini muffins

Estimate each product. Round the three-digit factor to the nearest hundred, and then multiply.

Mrs. Wu makes balloon animals. She buys 3 bags of balloons with 182 balloons in each bag. About how many balloons does Mrs. Wu buy?

_____ × _____ is about _____ × _____ = _____ balloons

The Gaston Theater sold 320 tickets each night for 5 nights. About how many tickets did the theater sell in all?

_____ × _____ is about _____ × _____ = _____ tickets

DAY 38: Complete sentences

A **sentence** is a group of words that forms a complete thought.

- A **complete sentence** has both a subject and a verb.
- A **sentence fragment** is a group of words that does not express a complete thought. It is often missing a subject or a verb.
- A **run-on sentence** is made up of two sentences that are joined without end punctuation or with just a comma.

Label each group of words as a complete sentence (C), a fragment (F), or a run-on sentence (R). Write the answers on the lines.

C	The cat is sleeping on the windowsill.	_____	Because it was storming.
_____	Her violin solo left the audience speechless.	_____	He likes pizza it's not his favorite food.
_____	While we were playing outside.	_____	I finished my breakfast, I helped clean up.
_____	Our dog barked loudly it scared the neighbors.	_____	He likes to read books and ride his bike.
_____	Her favorite color and her favorite fruit.	_____	My mom's dropping me off, I'm getting my hair cut.
_____	Adopted a dog and named her Teena.	_____	Since we had so many lemons, we made some lemonade.

Choose one of the sentence fragments or run-on sentences above, and rewrite it as a complete sentence on the lines below.

_____

_____

Day 39: Animal adaptations

An **adaptation** is an inherited trait that helps an organism survive or reproduce. For example, a giraffe's long, upright neck is an adaptation. This adaptation helps the giraffe reach leaves that are up high on trees.

Draw lines to match each adaptation to its main benefit.

Adaptation	Benefit
 green scales	This adaptation helps an animal stay warm.
 flat, webbed feet	This adaptation helps protect an animal from a predator with sharp teeth.
 thick, furry coat	This adaptation helps an animal camouflage among green leaves.
 hard outer shell	This adaptation helps an animal collect nectar from flowers.
 sharp teeth	This adaptation helps an animal swim easily through water.
 long, thin beak	This adaptation helps an animal tear through meat.

DAY 39: Area

Multiply to find the area of each rectangle.

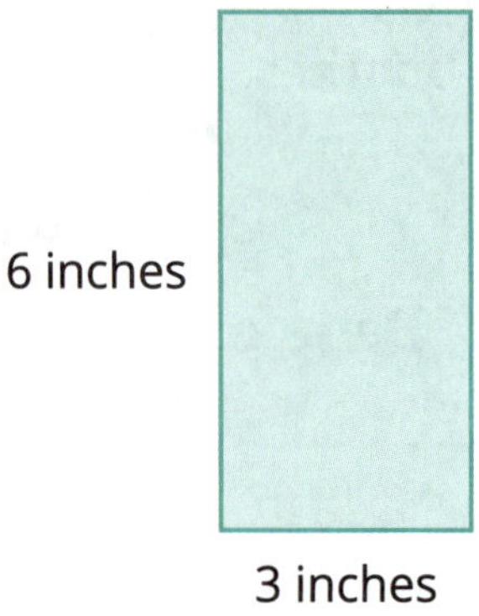

6 inches / 3 inches

_____ square inches

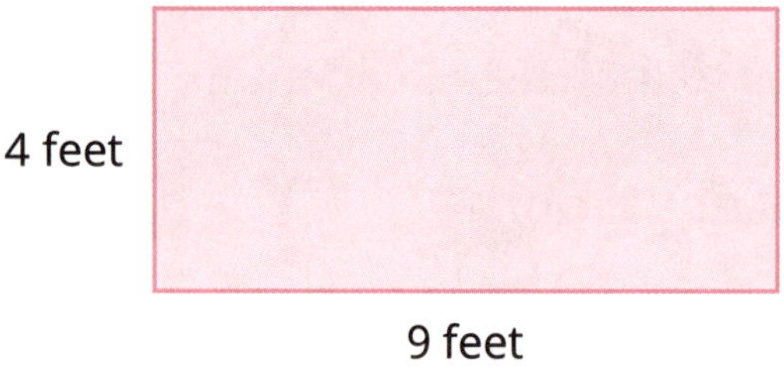

4 feet / 9 feet

_____ square feet

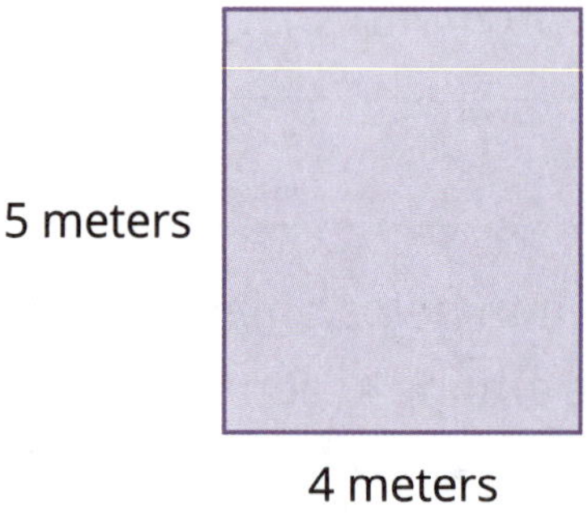

5 meters / 4 meters

_____ square meters

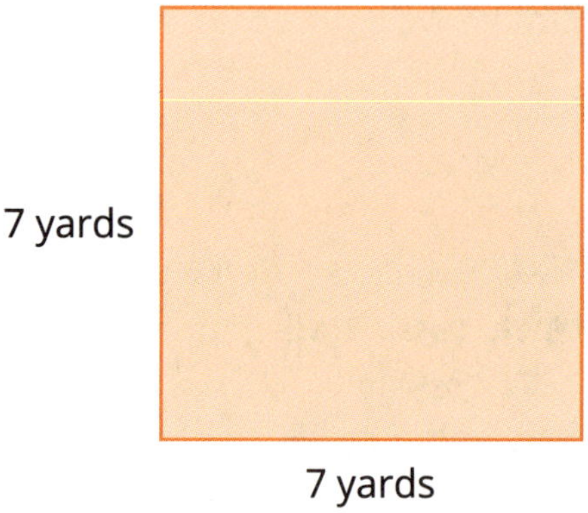

7 yards / 7 yards

_____ square yards

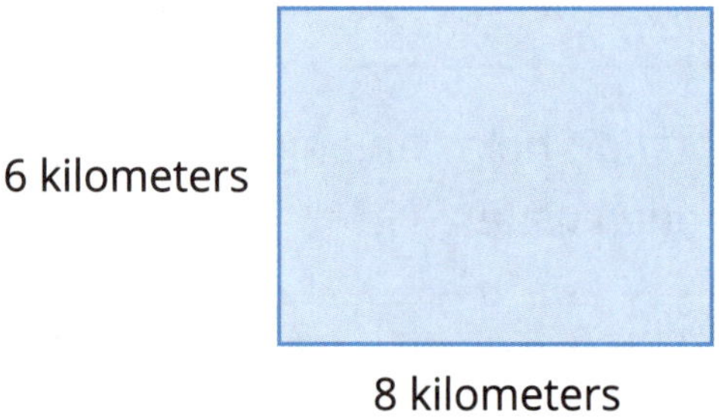

6 kilometers / 8 kilometers

_____ square kilometers

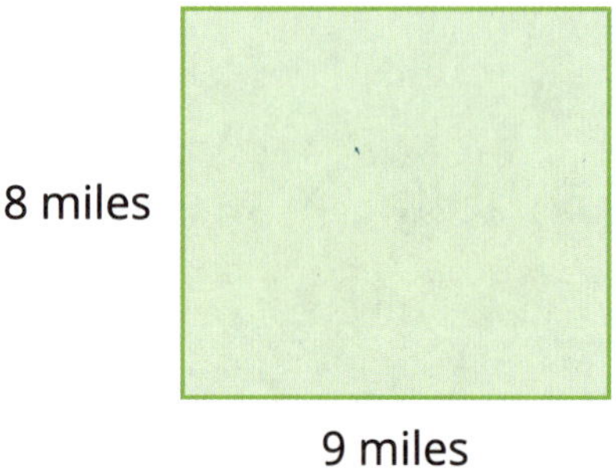

8 miles / 9 miles

_____ square miles

Analogies

An **analogy** shows how two things are related to each other. When solving analogies, look for a pattern between pairs of objects. Look at this example:

 is to  as 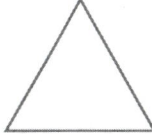 is to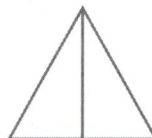

In this analogy, you draw a line down the middle to get from the first shape to the second shape.

Complete each analogy below by drawing the final shape.

 is to  as  is to _____

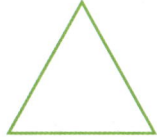 is to  as  is to _____

 is to  as  is to _____

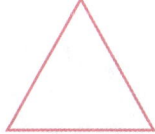 is to 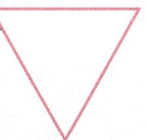 as  is to _____

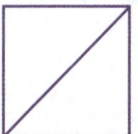 is to  as  is to _____

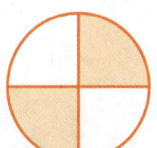 is to 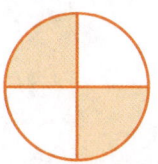 as  is to _____

ENRICHMENT

DAY 40: Name art

Create a design that represents you! First, think of your hobbies and interests. What are some of your favorite things? Brainstorm a list in the space below.

Next, use a pencil to lightly sketch the letters of your name in the space below. Form each letter with objects that represent you. Be sure to include details, and then add color!

N　　A　　M　　E

ENRICHMENT

DAY 41 Area

Find the area of each shape by adding the areas of the smaller rectangles.

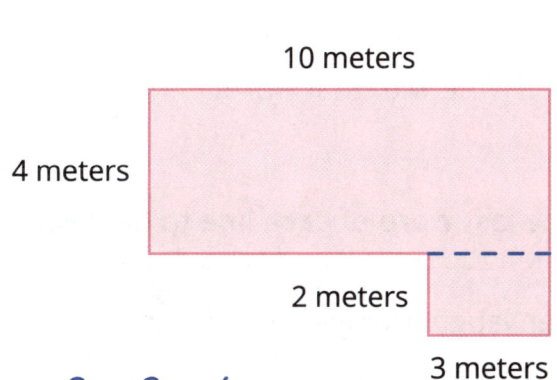

2 × 3 = 6
4 × 10 = 40

__6__ + __40__ = __46__ square meters

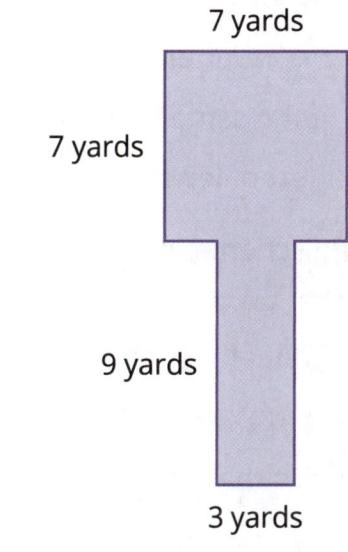

____ + ____ = ____ square yards

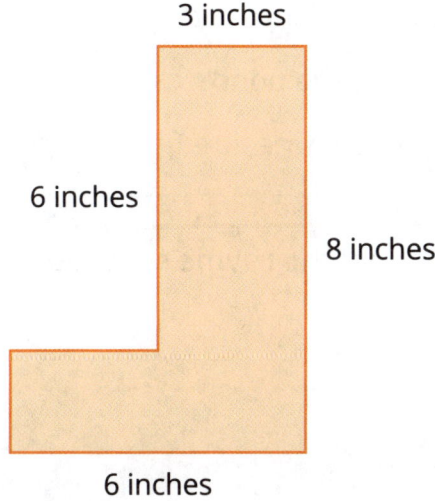

____ + ____ = ____ square inches

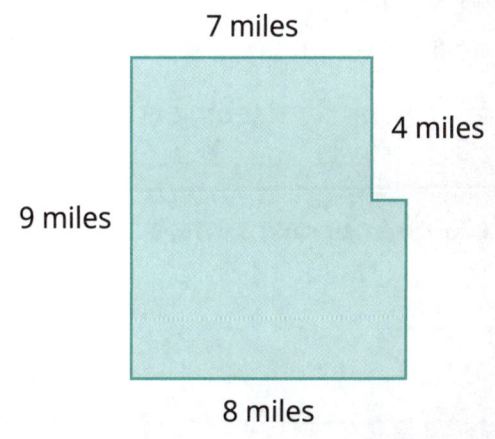

____ + ____ = ____ square miles

Brain Break! Stand up and stretch out your arms and legs like a starfish. With your right hand, reach down and touch your left foot. Stand back up, and then touch your left hand to your right foot. Alternate for a count of twenty!

Rhyme scheme

Rhyming words are often found at the ends of lines in a poem. A poem's rhymes form a pattern called a **rhyme scheme**. You can label the rhyme scheme with letters.

- Start with the letter A.
- Then use the same letter for other words that rhyme with that word.
- Use a different letter for each new rhyme.

Label the rhyme scheme in each poem. Underline the last word of each line to help you.

In the forest, deep and green,	A	Children laugh with glee and delight.	___
The tallest trees we've ever seen.	A	Fireworks boom in the sky,	___
Leaves whisper in the breeze,	B	Pink and yellow, orange and white.	___
Branches sway with gentle ease.	B	Summer drifts joyfully by.	___
The ocean waves are dark and blue,	___	Tiny dragons on jewel-bright wings,	___
The moon shines down a silver hue.	___	As willows dance with grace.	___
On deck, the captain gazes out.	___	All to kiss the pond's calm face,	___
Below, a soundly sleeping crew.	___	This simple treasure fit for kings.	___

Now create your own! Write a four-line poem and label the rhyme scheme.

DAY 42 Multiply using grids

Multiply using the grids. Each grid is split into two smaller parts. Follow the example.

6 × 23 = (6 × __20__) + (6 × __3__)

    = __120__ + __18__

    = __138__

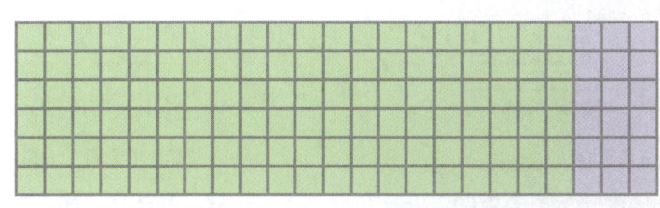

3 × 19 = (3 × _____) + (3 × _____)

    = _____ + _____

    = _____

5 × 17 = (5 × _____) + (5 × _____)

    = _____ + _____

    = _____

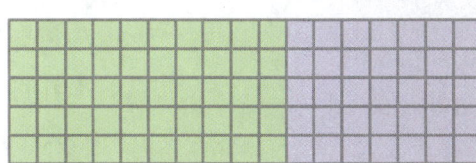

8 × 26 = (8 × _____) + (8 × _____)

    = _____ + _____

    = _____

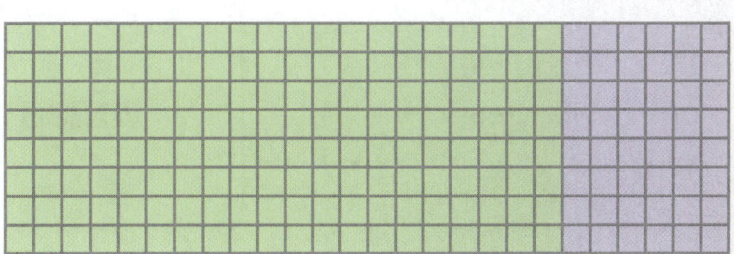

DAY 42: Pronouns

Find the path from start to finish. Move in the direction of the correct missing pronoun until you reach the end.

START: Lily and ___ went jogging in the park.
— I → Both Jack's painting and ___ are in the summer art fair!
— my → ___ will be fixing Serenity's old bike this weekend.

Down from START: myself → I earned enough money to buy the ticket ___.
Down from "Both Jack's painting": mine → The younger kids all laughed at ___ silly magic tricks.
Down from "will be fixing Serenity's": mine → Noah invited my sister and ___ to play basketball.

"I earned enough money" — me → "The younger kids" — my → "Noah invited my sister"

Down from "I earned enough money": my → These sunglasses aren't Taylor's or ___.
Down from "The younger kids": mine → Aunt Jane threw a surprise party for my cousin and ___.
Down from "Noah invited my sister": me → I made ___ a delicious breakfast this morning.

"These sunglasses" — I → "Aunt Jane threw" — myself → "I made ___ a delicious breakfast"

Down from "These sunglasses": myself → I like extra fudge on ___ ice cream sundae.
Down from "Aunt Jane threw": me → **FINISH**
Down from "I made": I → The coach asked ___ to help Charlotte practice.

"I like extra fudge" — I → **FINISH** — mine → "The coach asked"

DAY 43: Multiply using grids

IXL.com skill ID **8UH**

Multiply. Split each grid into two smaller parts to help you.

4 × 15 = (4 × _____) + (4 × _____)

   = _____ + _____

   = _____

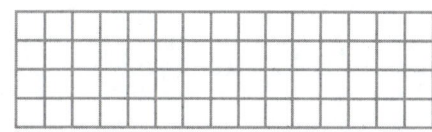

5 × 22 = (5 × _____) + (5 × _____)

   = _____ + _____

   = _____

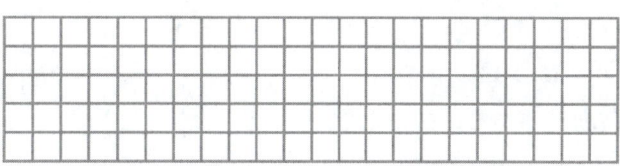

6 × 16 = (6 × _____) + (6 × _____)

   = _____ + _____

   = _____

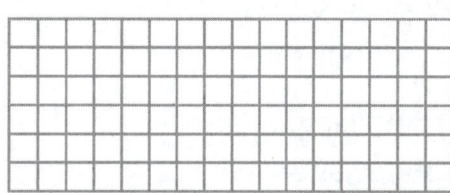

4 × 24 = (4 × _____) + (4 × _____)

   = _____ + _____

   = _____

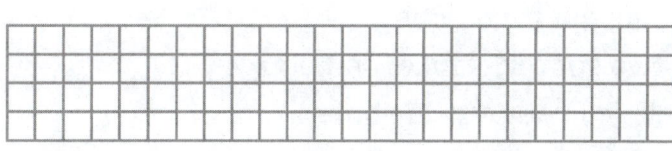

Day 43: Reading poetry

Read the poem and answer the questions. Write your answer on the lines, or put an X next to the correct answer.

A Well-Deserved Rest

You go on without me,
I'll sit this one out.
If I climb one more tree,
I think I might shout!

We've played forty-three games
Of various sports,
With so many names
And on all kinds of courts.

We've gone for twenty-six swims,
Mile-long walks in the damp.
We went to all kinds of gyms,
Even tried tennis camp!

Hiking and biking,
Every Sunday a run.
I can't take any more!
I've had it. I'm done.

I won't be leaving my nook,
No, not for a dime.
I've got my blanket and book—
Enjoy your outside time!

Who do you think the speaker is talking to in this poem? How do you know?

_____

_____

_____

What does "No, not for a dime" mean in the poem?

_____

_____

_____

Go back and label the rhyme scheme in the first stanza. What is the pattern?

_____

Which word best describes the tone of the poem?

____ angry   ____ bored

____ playful   ____ serious

What words, phrases, and techniques from the poem help create the tone?

_____

_____

_____

Opinion writing

DAY 44

IXL.com skill ID **MJN**

Plan and write a paragraph to respond to the prompt below. Complete the table to organize your thoughts. Then write your paragraph on the lines provided. Include transition words to connect your ideas.

Would you rather shrink to the size of an ant or grow to the size of a two-story building? Why?

Opinion statement *says what you believe, think, or feel about something*	
Reason *tells why you have the opinion*	
Example *supports your reason*	
Conclusion *restates your opinion*	

LANGUAGE ARTS

DAY 44: Landmarks and monuments

IXL.com skill ID **6FQ**

Use the clues to name each American landmark and monument.

> Capitol Building   Martin Luther King, Jr. Memorial   Jefferson Memorial
>
> Independence Hall   Empire State Building   Mount Rushmore

I honor a civil rights leader in Washington, D.C. What am I?

I once was the tallest building in New York City. What am I?

I show four presidents carved into a mountain in South Dakota. What am I?

I'm where the Declaration of Independence was signed in Philadelphia. What am I?

I'm where Congress meets to make laws in Washington, D.C. What am I?

I honor the writer of the Declaration of Independence. What am I?

DAY 45: Decode the riddles

Solve the riddles. Write each letter of your answer on a line. You can use the secret code below to help you!

What is the best day of the week to go to the beach?   S U N D A Y
                                                        6 1 15 16 10 4

What word is always spelled wrong in the dictionary?   __ __ __ __ __
                                                       19 3 8 15 20

What do you call a fish with no eyes?   __ __ __ __
                                        10 17 6 7

Who's the leader of the pencil case?   __ __ __ __ __ __ __ __
                                       11 7 14 3 1 2 14 3

What kind of tree fits in your hand?   __ __ __ __ __ __ __ __
                                       10 12 10 2 13 11 3 14 14

Which building has the most stories?   __ __ __ __ __ __ __ __ __
                                       11 7 14 2 9 5 3 10 3 4

What do you call a bear with no teeth?   __ __ __ __ __ __ __ __ __
                                         10 20 1 13 13 4 5 14 10 3

What do you call a dinosaur with a large vocabulary?   __ __ __ __ __ __ __ __ __
                                                       10 11 7 14 6 10 1 3 1 6

1	2	3	4	5	6	7	8	9	10	11	12	13	14	15	16	17	18	19	20
U	L	R	Y	B	S	H	O	I	A	T	P	M	E	N	D	F	K	W	G

ENRICHMENT

DAY 45 Logic puzzle

Coach Bryant is planning for Saturday's basketball game. Each of the five starting players wears a different jersey number. Each player also plays a different position, meaning they each have a special job to do during the game.

Use the clues and the grid below to find out which jersey number goes with each position.

- Neither of the guards wears jersey number 3.
- The power forward wears a jersey with an even number.
- The center's jersey number is greater than 20.
- The point guard's jersey number is one less than the shooting guard's jersey number.

		Positions			
Jersey numbers		Point guard	Shooting guard	Small forward	Power forward	Center
	3					
	7					
	8					
	23					
	34					

The point guard wears jersey number _____.

The shooting guard wears jersey number _____.

The small forward wears jersey number _____.

The power forward wears jersey number _____.

The center wears jersey number _____.

ENRICHMENT

Weeks 10–12: Overview

Week 10

Math
Area model multiplication
Line plots

Language arts
Nonfiction text features
Editing
Greek and Latin roots

Science
Earth's features

Enrichment
Riddles
Magic squares

Week 11

Math
One-digit by two-digit multiplication
Line plots with fractions

Language arts
Informational writing
Drawing conclusions from a story
Adjectives and adverbs

Social studies
Timelines

Enrichment
Anagrams
Complete the pictures

Week 12

Math
One-step word problems
Two-step word problems

Language arts
Text structure
Subordinating conjunctions
Personal narrative writing

Science
Moon phases

Enrichment
Designing robots
Gratitude reflection

More ways to learn

Keep the learning going! Use these simple, exciting activities to help you stay active, curious, and creative during your summer break.

See how many activities you can do! Cross off each activity as you complete it.

Complete a jigsaw puzzle. 	Make up a story about an object in your home. 	Make a collage out of scrap paper. 
Write an autobiography of your life so far. 	Interview a family member or neighbor. 	Plan and perform a skit or play. 
Cook or bake something. 	Come up with new words for a song you know. 	Decorate your room. 

DAY 46 Reading comprehension

Read the passage from a book about trees. Then answer the questions. Write your answer on the lines, or put an X next to the correct answer.

Redwood Trees

Redwood trees are the tallest living plants on Earth and can grow more than 300 feet tall. That's as tall as the Statue of Liberty!

The tallest redwoods live in northern California where there is plenty of fog. Redwoods have special leaves that can take in some of this water from the air, allowing the trees to grow taller than in other areas.

Surprisingly, a redwood's roots are only about 10 feet deep. A redwood grows its roots outward. The roots weave together with the roots of other redwoods in the area, allowing the trees to support one another.

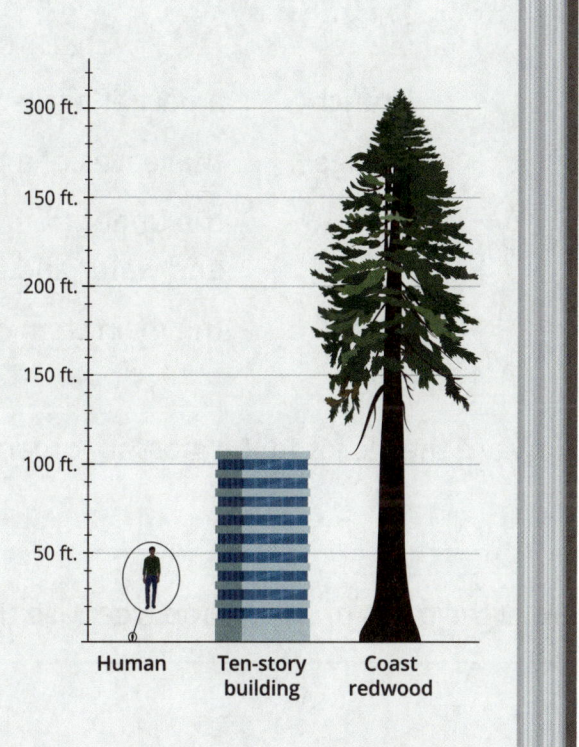

Why does the author mention the Statue of Liberty in the passage?

_____

How does the graph give readers a better understanding of redwood trees?

_____

_____

How do a redwood's leaves help the tree grow taller?

____ by weaving together with other redwoods

____ by giving the roots more shade

____ by taking in water from the air

DAY 46 Reading comprehension

A **glossary** tells you what some of the words in a book mean.

Read this glossary from a book about trees and answer the questions.

Glossary

branch	a part of a tree that grows from the trunk
foliage	the leaves of a plant
root	the underground part of a tree that collects nutrients and water and keeps the tree in the ground
trunk	the main stem of a tree

How are the words in the glossary organized?

_____

Label the parts of a redwood tree. Use the glossary to help you.

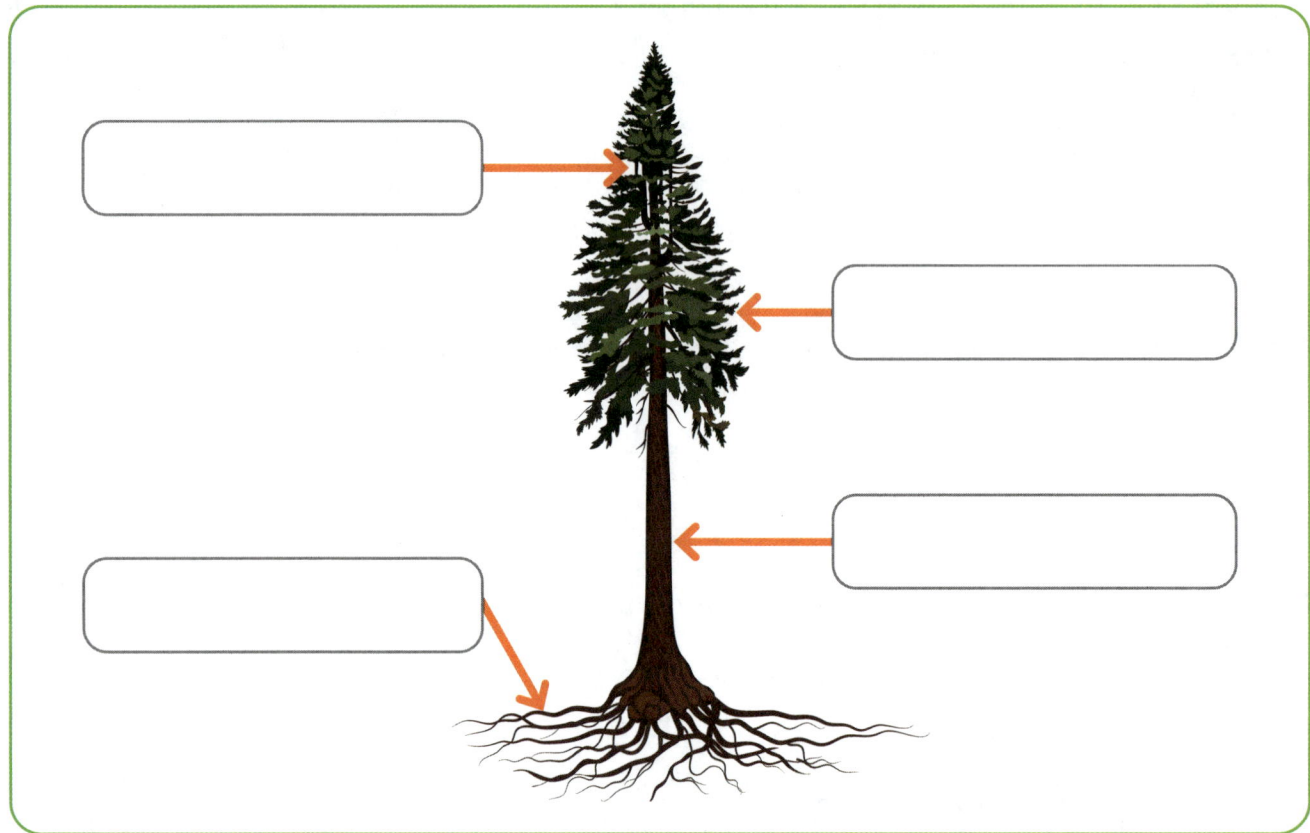

DAY 47: Multiply using area models

Multiply using the area models. Find the area of both parts of each model, and then add those areas.

4 × 23 = __92__

	20	3
4	80	12

__80__ + __12__ = __92__

---

6 × 42 = _____

	40	2
6	___	___

_____ + _____ = _____

---

5 × 67 = _____

	60	7
5	___	___

_____ + _____ = _____

---

8 × 79 = _____

	70	9
8	___	___

_____ + _____ = _____

DAY 47: Multiply using area models

Multiply using the area models.

3 × 85 = _____

_____ + _____ = _____

7 × 94 = _____

_____ + _____ = _____

6 × 73 = _____

_____ + _____ = _____

9 × 36 = _____

_____ + _____ = _____

DAY 48 Editing

Read each paragraph and find the spelling, punctuation, capitalization, and grammar errors. Cross out each error and write the correction above it. Use ^ to insert a word or punctuation mark.

How did people keep ~~there~~ *their* homes cool before modern air conditioning *?* For thousands of years, people a^round the world have built houses out of mud to beat the heat.

Mud bricks are made of earth, water, and straw. They soak up the heat of the son, while the inside of the building stay cool.

Natural caves usually stay cool, to. In one tiny Spanish town, people builded walls into the sides of rocky cliffs to make cave-like buildings. summers are hot and dry, but the homes in the rocks stay Nice and cool

In 1915, miners in australia needed a weigh to stay cool while searching for gold and gems. It was 120°F outside, and they found relief in the holes they dug. Soon, they turned those underground wholes into homes and called them dugouts Even today, the dugouts stay an lovely 75°F all year long.

Brain Break! Get a pencil and a piece of blank paper. Set a timer for three minutes and start doodling. Let your pencil draw whatever lines or shapes come to mind!

DAY 48 — Earth's features

IXL.com skill ID
KVM

Earth has many different natural land and water features. These features come in many shapes and sizes and can be found all around the world.

Complete the crossword puzzle. Each clue describes one land or water feature. Use the clues and the word bank to help you.

Word bank

Land features
- canyon
- island
- mountain
- plain
- valley
- volcano

Water features
- lake
- pond
- ocean
- river
- waterfall

Across

3. A deep and narrow landform, with steep cliffs on both sides
5. A wide, mostly flat area of land without many trees
7. A small body of water with land all around it
8. An opening in the ground where gases and melted rock can reach Earth's surface
11. A low area of land between mountains or hills

Down

1. A piece of land that is fully surrounded by water
2. A large landform that rises high above the surrounding land
4. Water that falls down from a high place
6. Water that moves in a line across land
9. A large inland body of water
10. One of the five large bodies of salt water that cover most of the Earth's surface

DAY 49 Line plots

Jabari recorded the daily high temperature for each day in July. He recorded the data on the line plot below.

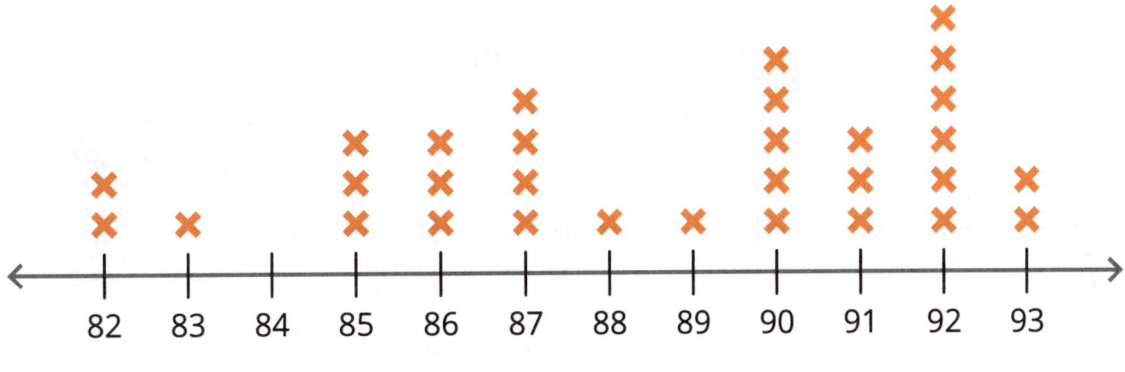

High temperatures in July

Temperature (in °F)
Each ✗ = 1 day

Answer each question.

What was the greatest high temperature? _____ °F

How many days had a high temperature of 86°F? _____ days

How many days had a high temperature 90°F or greater? _____ days

How many more days had a high temperature of 92°F than 82°F? _____ more days

DAY 49: Greek and Latin roots

IXL.com skill ID **TE5**

A **root** is a part of a word that has a certain meaning. Words that share the same root often have similar meanings that are related to the meaning of the root.

auto: own or self	**bio:** life	**geo:** earth or rock
graph: write or draw	**logy:** the study of something	**micro:** small
phon: sound	**scope:** look at or observe	**tele:** far away

Draw lines to match each word with its definition. Use the root word meanings above to help you.

- autograph
- biography
- geology
- graphology
- microbiology
- microscope
- telephone
- telescope

- the study of someone's handwriting
- the study of very small life forms
- a person's signature written in his or her own handwriting
- a written account of a person's life
- a device that can carry the sound of someone's voice somewhere far away
- the study of Earth's history, especially as recorded in rocks
- a tool used to look at something that is far away
- a tool used to look at something too small to see with just your eyes

DAY 50: Hink pinks

A **hink pink** is a riddle whose answer is a pair of rhyming one-syllable words.

Read each clue below and write the correct answer in the space provided. Remember, each answer will be two one-syllable words that rhyme.

What do you call a dog after it goes swimming?	wet pet
What do you call a fearless ocean greeting?	
What do you call a slightly wet group of tents?	
What do you call a tight hug from a gentle wind?	
What do you call the scent of a hermit crab's home?	
What do you call a story told by a giant ocean mammal?	
What is it called when you give a talk on a sandy shore?	
What do you call a group of instruments playing music on the beach?	
What do you call a dessert that someone eats while visiting a large body of fresh water?	

Day 50: Magic squares

Fill in the missing numbers to complete the magic squares! Each row, column, and diagonal should add up to the given total.

The total is 18.

7	8	3
2	6	10
9	4	5

The total is 27.

12	5	10
7	9	11
8	13	6

The total is 51.

16	15	20
21	17	13
14	19	18

The total is 90.

27	34	29
32	30	28
31	26	33

Become an IXL member for unlimited practice. Join today! Scan the QR code or visit www.ixl.com/workbook/34s for details.

DAY 51
Multiply using area models

Multiply. Draw area models to help.

$3 \times 67 =$ __201__

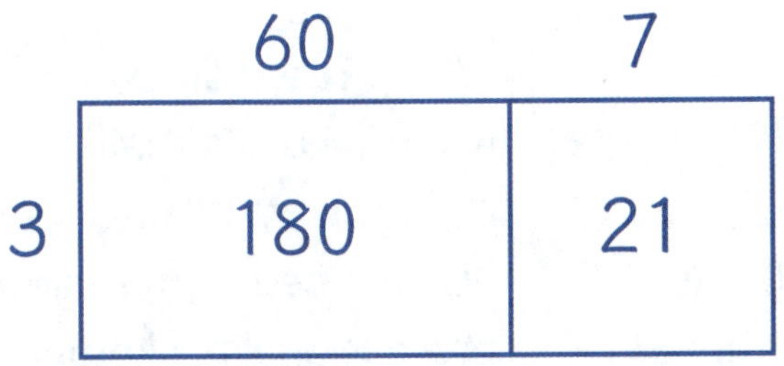

	60	7
3	180	21

180 + 21 = 201

$4 \times 83 =$ _____

$6 \times 68 =$ _____

$7 \times 47 =$ _____

$9 \times 72 =$ _____

$8 \times 59 =$ _____

DAY 51

Timelines

IXL.com skill ID **FYY**

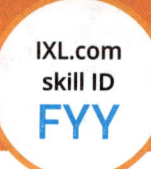

Use the timeline to answer each question. Write your answer on the lines, or put an X next to the correct answer.

History of Basketball

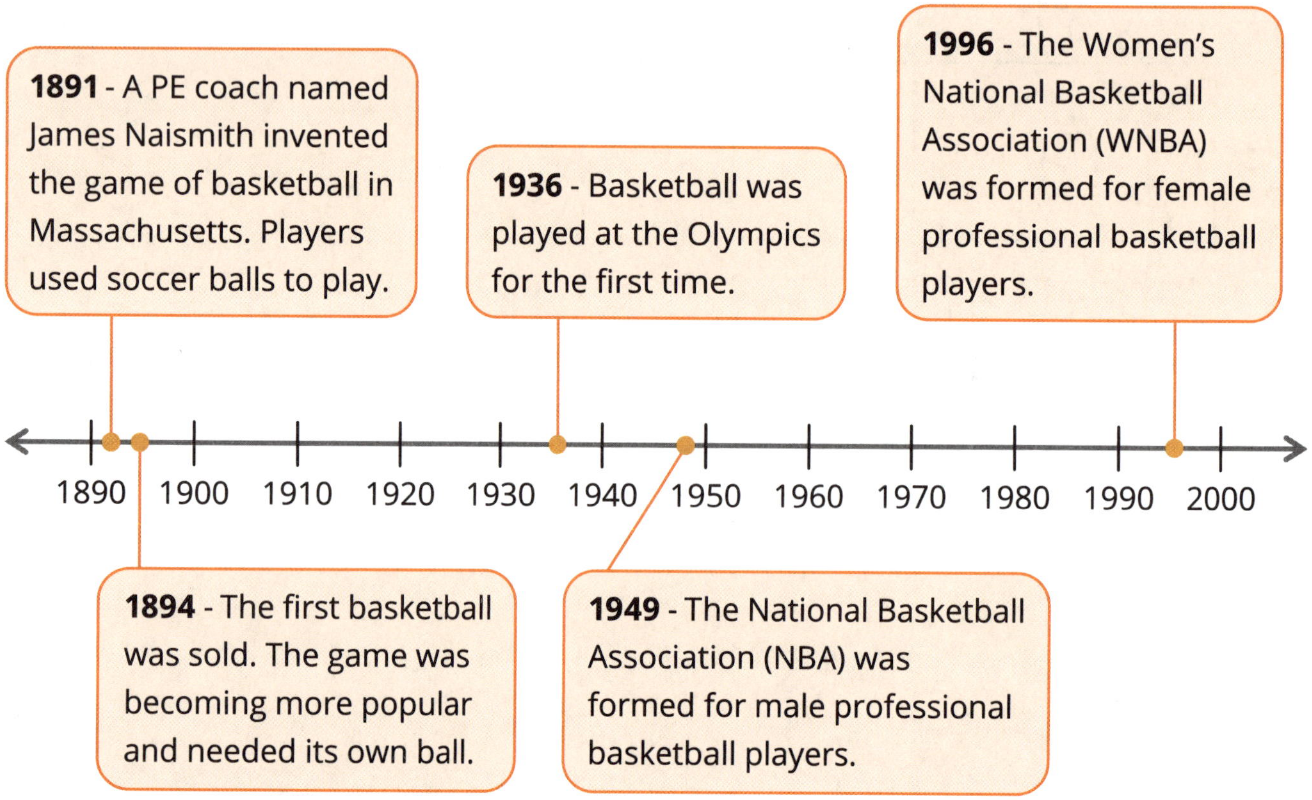
1891 - A PE coach named James Naismith invented the game of basketball in Massachusetts. Players used soccer balls to play.
1936 - Basketball was played at the Olympics for the first time.
1996 - The Women's National Basketball Association (WNBA) was formed for female professional basketball players.
1890
1900
1910
1920
1930
1940
1950
1960
1970
1980
1990
2000
1894 - The first basketball was sold. The game was becoming more popular and needed its own ball.
1949 - The National Basketball Association (NBA) was formed for male professional basketball players.

When was basketball first played? ____________

When was the first basketball sold? ____________

Which was formed first, the NBA or the WNBA? ____________

For how many years was basketball around before it was played at the Olympics for the first time? ____________ years

Which happened more recently?

____ Basketball was first played at the Olympics.

____ The WNBA was formed.

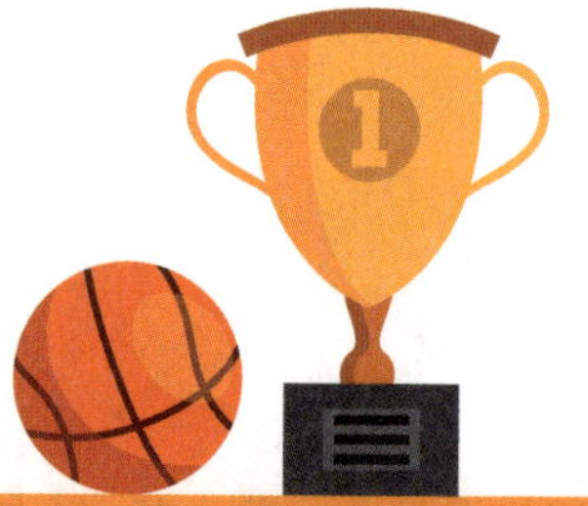

DAY 52: Informational writing

Plan and write a paragraph to respond to the prompt below. Complete the table to organize your thoughts. Then write your paragraph on the lines provided. Include transition words to connect your ideas.

> Write about a topic that you know a lot about. You might explain how to play a game you love, tell about your favorite hobby, or share details about a person you admire. Focus on facts rather than opinions.

Topic sentence *tells the reader what the paragraph is about*			
Key details *give more information about the topic*			
Conclusion *sums up the information*			

_____

_____

_____

_____

LANGUAGE ARTS

DAY 52: Tic-tac-toe multiplication

Find the row, column, or diagonal where all of the products are the same. You can draw area models to help you.

8 × 29 = _____	2 × 85 = _____	6 × 39 = _____
5 × 67 = _____	3 × 78 = _____	7 × 59 = _____
9 × 26 = _____	6 × 42 = _____	4 × 57 = _____

Get ahead of the curve with extra practice! Join IXL today. Visit www.ixl.com/workbook/34s for details.

Reading comprehension

Read the first part of the story below. Then answer the questions.

Curiosity and the Cat

"Pass it here!" shouted Sofía as she raced down the field. José kicked the soccer ball to his sister, but just as Sofía went to kick it, she noticed something odd sticking out of the grass.

"What's that?" she asked, bending down to get a closer look. "It's like Abuela's TV remote." She picked up the small metal device covered with colorful buttons.

José approached his sister. "Be careful, Sofía, we don't know what that thing does."

Never one to hesitate, Sofía grinned and said, "Well, there's one way to find out." Before José could stop her, Sofía jammed her finger down on a big red button.

Suddenly, a beam of white light shot from the device. Sofía dropped the strange object as both children covered their eyes with their arms. When the light faded, everything looked...bigger.

They found themselves surrounded by tall green columns. It was the grass, they realized after a moment. "Sofía, we shrank!" gasped José in shock.

Nearby, they could see their soccer ball. "This is amazing!" laughed Sofía. "The soccer ball is as big as a house! I bet it would take ten of us to move that thing."

Just then, a loud rumble made the ground shake. It sounded like an elephant was charging toward them. "I don't have a good feeling about this..." José said.

In the text, underline the details that help readers picture the setting after the children shrink.

What do you think is coming toward the children? Explain your prediction.

_____

_____

Reading comprehension

Read the next part of the story. Then answer the questions.

Suddenly a tabby cat appeared, an enormous striped monster stomping across the grass. Its huge green eyes were fixed curiously on the children. Sofía froze in terror. "José, what are we going to do?" she whispered. José grabbed Sofía's wrist and quickly pulled her under a nearby fallen leaf.

Peeking out, Sofía trembled as the playful cat began swatting at a leaf near the one they were under. José knew they needed to quickly return to their actual size before the cat found them. "The remote! We have to hit the button!" he said. But how could they do that? The metal remote was twice their height, with nothing but rounded edges. There weren't even places to hold onto for climbing.

The cat came closer, and they held onto a corner of their leaf to keep covered. Suddenly, the cat grabbed their leaf shelter in its mouth. As they flew through the air, José caught sight of the buttons just below them and got a crazy idea. "Sofía, jump!" yelled José, grasping his sister's hand. They let go of the leaf and landed heavily on a big blue button. In a flash of light, they were back to normal, while the confused cat hurried away.

José and Sofía looked at each other and then down at the strange device. "Maybe we should be more careful about what we touch from now on," laughed José with relief. Sofía just nodded in agreement. Adventure was good, but some mysteries were best left unsolved.

Read each description. Write a J if it describes José and an S if it describes Sofía.

_____ is curious   _____ is protective

_____ thinks quickly under pressure   _____ freezes under pressure

In your own words, tell what lesson the characters learn in this story.

_____

Day 54: Line plots

The Allensburg Beach Museum has shark teeth on display. The line plot shows the lengths of the teeth in the display.

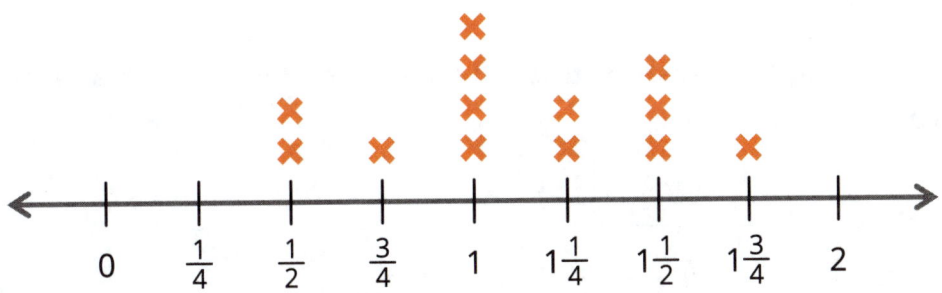

Answer each question.

How many 1-inch shark teeth are in the display? _____ shark teeth

How long is the longest shark tooth in the display? _____ inches long

How many more $1\frac{1}{2}$-inch shark teeth does the museum have on display than $\frac{3}{4}$-inch shark teeth? _____ more shark teeth

How many shark teeth are on display in all? _____ shark teeth

Brain Break!  Go outside for a few minutes and quietly observe the world around you. What colors do you see? What movement do you notice? What sounds do you hear?

DAY 54: Adjectives and adverbs

An **adjective** is a word that describes a noun, while an **adverb** is a word that describes a verb.

In the sentences below, each adjective or adverb is **bolded**, and the word it describes is underlined.

Find the path from start to finish. Your path should go only through spaces with a bolded adverb.

START ⬇

- The fox moved **quickly** through the bushes. *(START)*
- Quinn's parents **proudly** clapped at the end of the play.
- You must try one of these **ripe** peaches!
- Alissa grabbed her **hockey** stick for practice.
- I spread out a **beach** blanket on the sand.
- Maya **eagerly** climbs up on the horse's back.
- We **easily** completed the puzzles in less than an hour.
- During the repair work, our street was **bumpy**.
- Let's move some of these **cardboard** boxes.
- The stone was **perfect** for skipping across the lake.
- Dawson tries **hard** to make his brother laugh.
- The weather was **lovely** during our trip to Connecticut.
- Hugo walked **nervously** backstage to get into place. *(FINISH)*
- My dog **rarely** misses a chance to earn a treat.
- Gia **correctly** guessed how many pennies were in the jar.
- After the **rainy** morning, we jumped in lots of puddles.

FINISH

DAY 55 Anagrams

Anagrams are words or phrases made by rearranging the letters of another word or phrase.

Unscramble each anagram using the categories as clues.

Trees

lamp: _palm_
raced: _cedar_
ample: _maple_

Farm animals

balm: _____
toga: _____
shore: _____

Fruit

mile: _____
cheap: _____
among: _____

Ways to travel

arc: _____
panel: _____
in art: _____

Sports

flog: _____
in nets: _____
loaf bolt: _____

Found in a bakery

snub: _____
beard: _____
pack cues: _____

Challenge time! Unscramble each anagram and record the category name.

Category: _____

bolster: _____
carol: _____

hold pin: _____
scoot up: _____

ENRICHMENT

DAY 55
Complete the pictures

Complete the right side of each picture so that it is a mirror image of the left side.

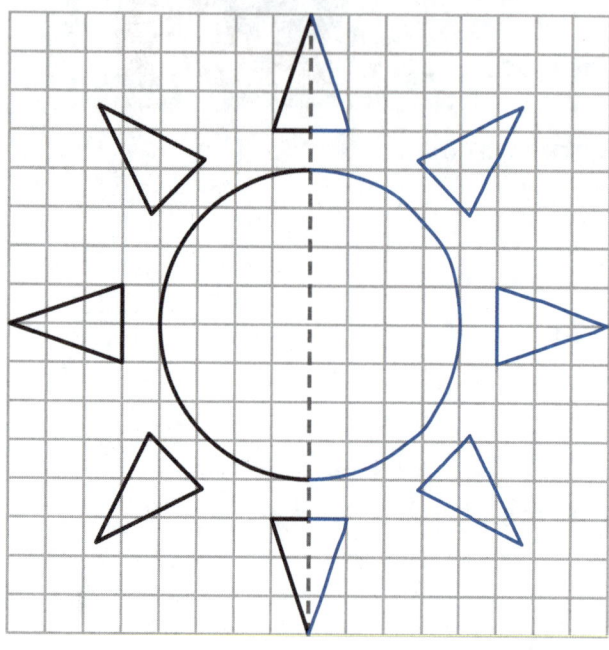
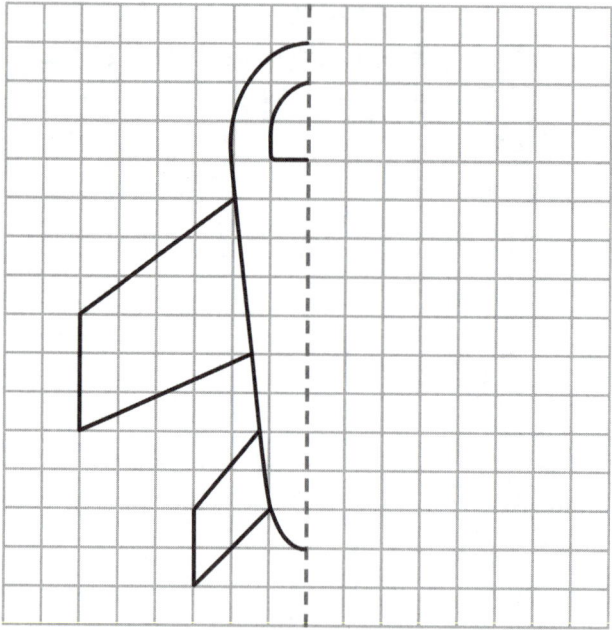
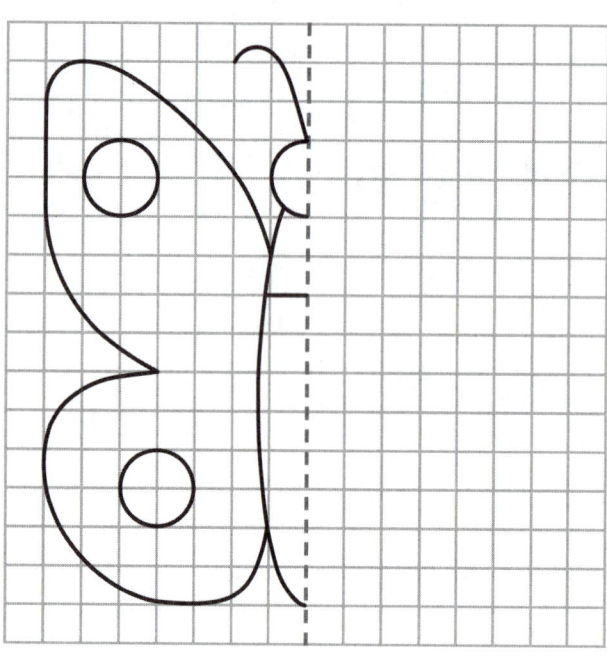
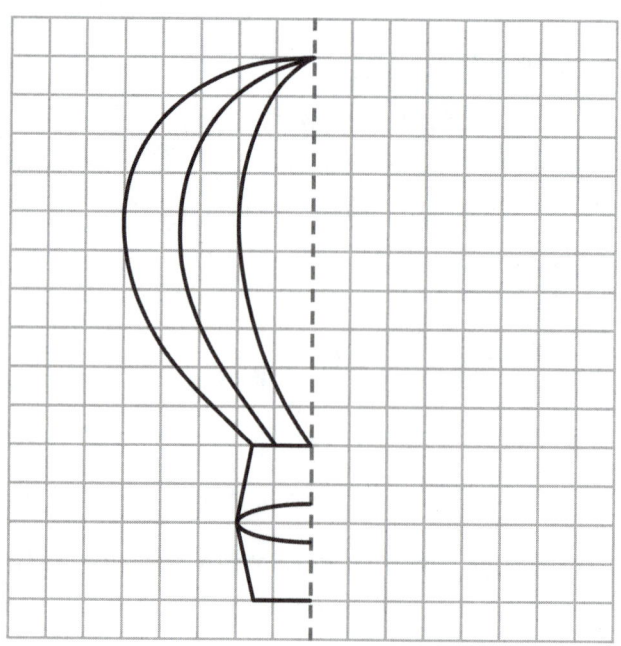

ENRICHMENT

DAY 56
Text structure

Writers use different **text structures** to organize their ideas. When you can tell how a text is organized, it's easier to understand how the writer's ideas go together. Look at some common text structures below:

- **Sequential** texts tell you about events that happen in a certain order.
- **Cause-effect** texts show the reasons for, and the results of, an event.
- **Problem-solution** texts explain a challenge and offer possible ways to solve it.
- **Compare-contrast** texts show how two or more things are the same or different.
- **Descriptive** texts tell you a list of details about an object, scene, or topic.

Read each description below. In the space provided, write the text structure the author should use to organize their ideas.

An author wants to instruct someone on the steps for building a bookcase.	sequential
An author wants to explain how stars and planets are similar and different.	
An author wants to give facts about the plants and animals in a state park.	
An author wants to tell what happens if you give a house plant too much water.	
An author wants to give ideas for how to keep squirrels from eating all the seeds you put out for the birds.	
An author wants to share the highlights from each day of a recent vacation to Iceland.	

DAY 56: Text structure

Read each paragraph below. Think about what the author is communicating and how the information is organized. Write the text structure used in each paragraph.

Keep cool by making a sweet frozen snack! Gather two bananas, two tablespoons of nut butter, and a handful of granola or chocolate chips. Start by slicing the bananas into round pieces. Then, cover the banana slices in the nut butter. Finish by rolling them in the granola, the chocolate chips, or both! Finally, put your treats on a plate, and place them in the freezer overnight. After twenty-four hours, take them out of the freezer and enjoy your tasty frozen banana bites!

Text structure:

Peaches and nectarines are similar fruits that first grew in China and now grow in many parts of the world. Both fruits have a similar reddish-orange color, but peaches have fuzzy skin while nectarines are smooth. Nectarines and peaches have pits in the middle and can be either yellow or white inside. Peaches tend to be a little bigger, and nectarines are usually firmer. No matter which one you prefer, nectarines and peaches are both delicious summer fruits.

Text structure:

Berries stay fresh for only a few weeks after being picked in the summer. So how can someone enjoy their sweet flavor year-round? One way to keep berries fresh is to store them in jugs of honey. Another trick is to dry berries in the sun so that they don't spoil. Heating the fruit and sealing it in jars to make jelly and jam is another way people can save and eat berries all year long. All of these methods of preserving berries allow people to delight in their flavor well beyond their season.

Text structure:

DAY 57 — Word problems

The Jackson family visits Sandmore Beach during their vacation. Answer each question.

The family builds 3 sandcastles and decorates them with seashells. They use 24 seashells on each sandcastle. How many seashells does the family use in all?

_____ seashells

The Jacksons buy 4 bags of taffy at a gift shop. Each bag has 48 pieces of taffy in it. How many pieces of taffy does the family buy in all?

_____ pieces of taffy

All 6 members of the family decide to rent bikes for the day. Bike rentals cost $26 a day. What is the total cost of the bike rentals?

_____

The Jackson family packs 7 water bottles for their bike ride. Each water bottle has 22 ounces of water. How many ounces of water do they bring on the ride in all?

_____ ounces

Brain Break! Find a place to sit or lie down. Squeeze all the muscles in your neck and shoulders for a count of five and release. Then tense and release your arms and hands. Now do the same for your back and stomach, followed by your legs and feet. How does your body feel now?

DAY 57: Subordinating conjunctions

A **subordinating conjunction** is a word that connects two simple sentences and gives information about the relationship between them. Some of the most common subordinating conjunctions are listed below.

after	because	unless
although	before	until
as	since	while

Circle the subordinating conjunction in each sentence.

(Before) the game starts, the players stretch and warm up.

Halle refused to sign up for the talent show unless Audrey signed up too.

While Grandpa boiled the pasta, Owen shredded the cheddar cheese.

We stayed inside and watched movies since it was raining all weekend.

Our dog Lucky loves going to the park because he gets to play with other dogs.

As he was pulling weeds in his garden, Joseph noticed the tiny snail.

Although the trail is steep, the view from the top is worth the effort.

I didn't know how to ride a bike until my aunt taught me last summer.

Write a sentence with each of the three subordinating conjunctions below.

after	
since	
unless	

DAY 58 Moon phases

IXL.com skill ID
XYF

A **moon phase** is the way the moon looks from Earth at different times during the month. Our view of the moon changes as it orbits, or goes around, Earth. We use special words to describe each phase.

A **full moon** is when the side of the moon that faces Earth is completely lit by the sun. That's when the moon looks like a full circle. A **new moon** is when none of the side of the moon that faces Earth is lit by the sun. That's when we can't see the moon.

Look at some other words used to describe the phases of the moon.

| **waxing:** getting bigger | **crescent:** shaped like a C | **quarter:** half full |
| **waning:** getting smaller | **gibbous:** almost full | |

Complete the names of the moon phases on the diagram. Use the vocabulary above and the word bank below to help you.

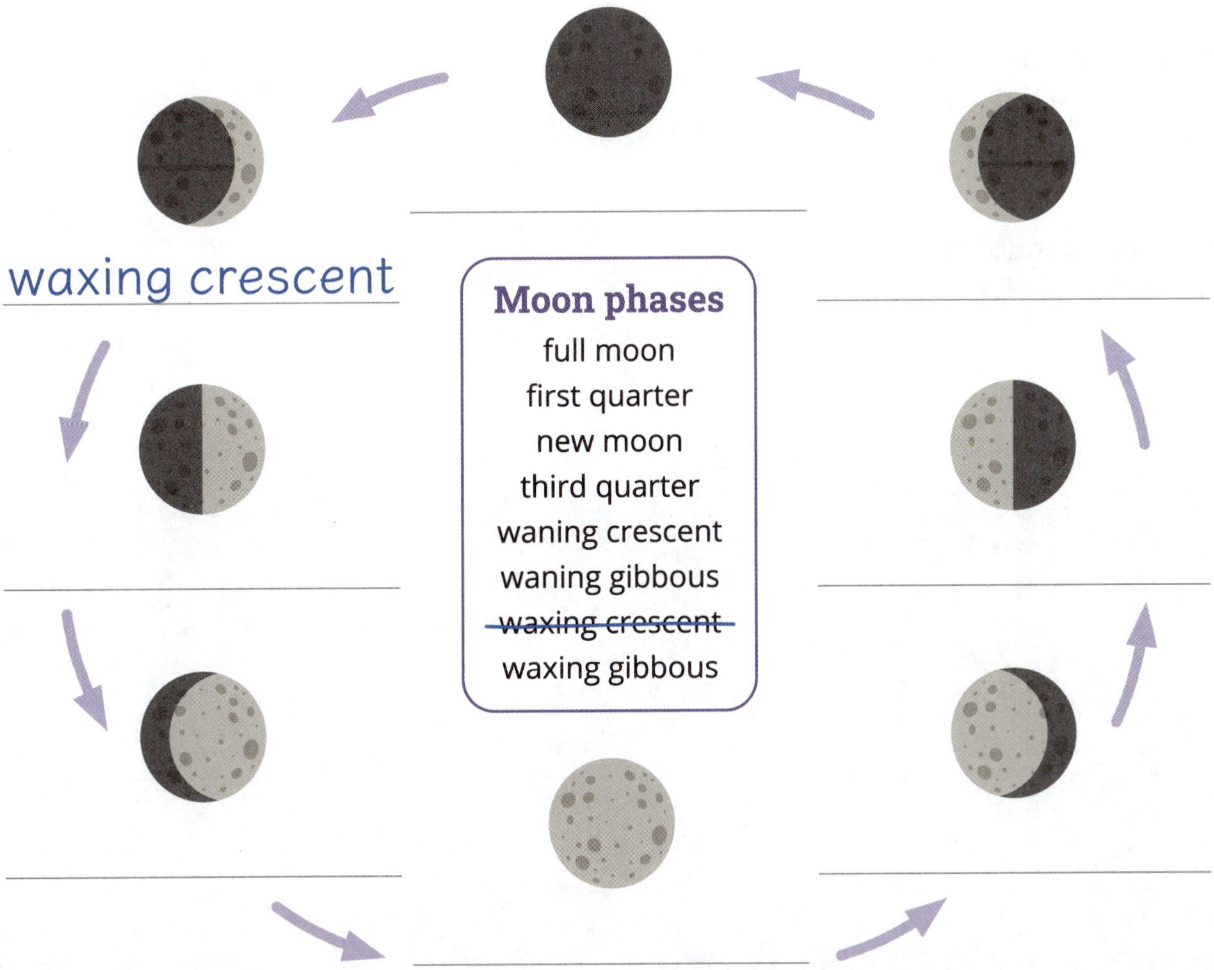

waxing crescent

Moon phases
full moon
first quarter
new moon
third quarter
waning crescent
waning gibbous
~~waxing crescent~~
waxing gibbous

SCIENCE
127
© IXL Learning

DAY 58: Personal narrative writing

IXL.com skill ID
SCZ

Plan and write a paragraph to respond to the prompt below. Complete the table to organize your thoughts. Then write your paragraph on the lines provided. Include transition words to connect your ideas.

Tell about a time when you overcame a challenge or helped somebody else overcome a challenge.		
Who was there?	When did it happen?	Where did it happen?
What happened first?		Details (thoughts, feelings, sights, sounds)
What happened next?		
What happened last?		

_____

_____

_____

_____

DAY 59: Word problems

The town of Plattsburgh holds a parade every year to celebrate the end of summer. Answer each question.

This year, 96 adults and 344 kids are marching in the parade. How many total people are marching in the parade?

_____ people

There are 13 floats in the parade with 8 people riding on each. How many total people are riding on the floats?

_____ people

On the left side of the street, there are 976 people watching the parade. On the right side, there are 894 people watching. How many more people are watching the parade on the left side of the street than on the right?

_____ more people

This year's parade includes 4 dance groups. Each group has 17 dancers. How many dancers are in the parade?

_____ dancers

There are 150 athletes and 126 marching band members marching in the parade. How many more athletes are there than marching band members?

_____ more athletes

DAY 59 Word problems

IXL.com skill ID
TFH

Keep going! Answer each question about the Plattsburgh end-of-summer parade.

The local art club has 550 lollipops and 370 candy bars to throw into the crowd during the parade. Art club members throw 872 pieces of candy into the crowd. How many pieces of candy do they have left after the parade?

_____ pieces of candy

Volunteers at the library buy water bottles to give out. They set up 6 stations with 85 water bottles at each. They set up 2 more stations with 95 water bottles at each. How many water bottles are at the stations in all?

_____ water bottles

Lara takes pictures of the parade for the local newspaper. She takes 106 pictures of people marching in the parade, 93 pictures of floats, and 172 pictures of people in the crowd. How many pictures does Lara take in all?

_____ pictures

Volunteers from the senior center give away 300 balloons. Each balloon is either red or gold. They give away all of the 150 red balloons. They have 11 gold balloons left over at the end of the parade. How many gold balloons did they give away?

_____ gold balloons

Boost your learning and save 20%. Join IXL today! Visit www.ixl.com/workbook/34s for details.

130 © IXL Learning MATH

DAY 60 — Designing robots

Some friends are designing robots on grid paper! Read each description and complete the prompts.

Kelsey designed this robot. Help Kelsey find the area of each of the robot's parts. Then find the total area of the robot.

Area of head = _____ square units

Area of neck = _____ square units

Area of body = _____ square units

Area of arms = _____ square units

Area of legs = _____ square units

Total area = _____ square units

Help Elliot draw a robot with the given areas for each part. Then find the total area.

Area of head = 9 square units

Area of neck = 1 square units

Area of body = 6 square units

Area of arms = 6 square units

Area of legs = 12 square units

Total area = _____ square units

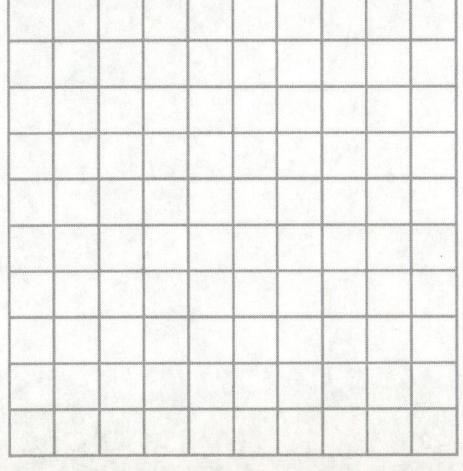

Help Maya draw a robot with a total area of 40 square units. Decide what the area of each part will be.

Area of head = _____ square units

Area of neck = _____ square units

Area of body = _____ square units

Area of arms = _____ square units

Area of legs = _____ square units

Total area = 40 square units

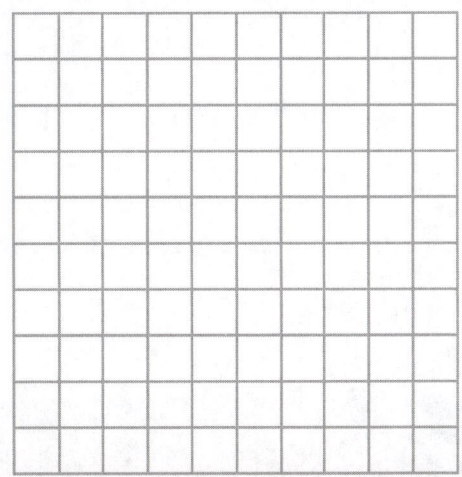

DAY 60: Gratitude reflection

Take a moment and reflect on some of your favorite people, places, and things. Use words or images to complete the table.

Someone who makes you laugh	Something that reminds you of home
Something that smells wonderful	A place where you like to spend time
Something that is your favorite color	Someone who makes you feel better
Something that you do to relax	Something that makes you special

Answer key

PAGE 7

985	232	337
701	235	937
882	47	683

```
  99 7       3 36       95 4
-  1 36    + 48 2     -  5 56
  ─────     ─────      ─────
   861       818         398

  58 6       81 3       14 7
+ 21 5     -  3 04    + 67 6
  ─────     ─────      ─────
   801       509         823
```

PAGE 8

*Alternate answer for 5-down: TREK
*Alternate answer for 9-down: MEDIAN

PAGE 9

When driving, you are free to stop and look around.

Strawberries can be grown in pots or in the ground.

Hats can help protect you from the sun.

Headphones make it harder to hear nearby traffic.

PAGE 10

983
348
206
475
624
129
862
133

PAGE 11

Sample answer: The people in the room likely feel excited. The text says that the air buzzed, and everyone was looking at the boxes on the tables.

Emma has never been to a jigsaw puzzle contest before.

PAGE 12

moving quickly

Emma and her dad like to do jigsaw puzzles together.

eager

PAGE 13

635 tubes

174 feet longer

534 lockers

971 visitors

159 chairs

PAGE 14

Clembury

Sonville

Noem River and Thorn River

Paisat

Bemfeld

PAGE 15

		Places				
		Briney Beach	Mirabella Mountains	Celia City	Thenway Theme Park	Historic Huntstown
Families	Morales family	X	X	●	X	X
	Baker family	X	X	X	X	●
	Chen family	X	●	X	X	X
	Taylor family	●	X	X	X	X
	Harris family	X	X	X	●	X

PAGE 16

wow, kayak, level

amazing, wonderful, great

pause, brake, rest

handlebar, pedal, wheel

airplane, boat, car

PAGE 17

57	67	77	**87**	97	**107**	**117**
78	**79**	**80**	81	82	83	**84**
220	**320**	420	520	**620**	720	**820**

1,154	1,155	**1,156**	1,157	1,158	**1,159**	**1,160**
600	1,600	2,600	**3,600**	**4,600**	**5,600**	6,600
4,752	4,852	**4,952**	5,052	5,152	**5,252**	**5,352**
1,996	1,997	1,998	**1,999**	**2,000**	2,001	**2,002**

PAGE 18

RED pre- GREEN -able
ORANGE re- BLUE -ful
YELLOW mis- PURPLE -less

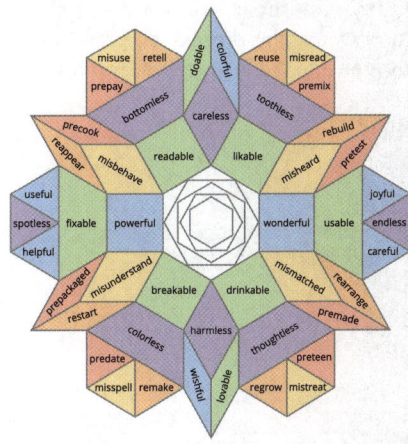

PAGE 19

5,726	6,231
2,943	5,465
8,154	1,078
3,617	4,809

4,836 = 4,000 + **800** + 30 + **6**

1,694 = 1,000 + 600 + **90** + 4

6,522 = 6,000 + **500** + 20 + **2**

5,714 = **5,000** + **700** + 10 + **4**

8,765 = **8,000** + 700 + 60 + **5**

3,953 = 3,000 + **900** + **50** + 3

2,381 = **2,000** + **300** + **80** + 1

9,299 = **9,000** + 200 + **90** + 9

PAGE 20

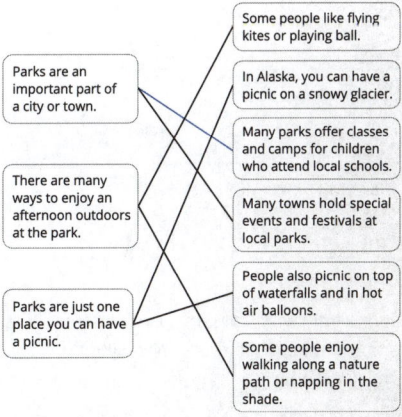

Answers will vary. A sample answer is shown below.

Parks have different things to see and enjoy.

Answer key

PAGE 21

Photosynthesis is a process in which plants use energy from **sunlight** to make their own food. Plants use **carbon dioxide** from the air and **water** from the soil to make **sugar**, which plants use as food. During this process, plants release **oxygen** into the air as a waste product.

PAGE 22

6,473	7,552	5,389
3,123	7,590	6,357
6,177	3,348	7,145

```
  3,729      7,463      4,281
+ 4,513    - 1,820    + 3,650
  -----      -----      -----
  8,242      5,643      7,931

  5,419      5,814      7,402
+ 2,637    -   906    - 5,378
  -----      -----      -----
  8,056      4,908      2,024
```

PAGE 24

Some animals can quickly change their skin color to help them survive.

Cuttlefish are ocean animals like octopuses and squid.

Answers will vary. Some possible answers are shown below.

1.	to communicate with other animals
2.	to hide from predators or prey
3.	to control their body temperature

D
C
A
B

PAGE 25

Drawings will vary.

PAGE 26

Answers will vary.

PAGE 27

carefree

Sample answer: Rowan is probably feeling upset because he thinks Mr. Silver will be angry with him.

PAGE 28

unsure

Sample answer: Rowan probably feels nervous and frightened. He can't even talk as he faces Mr. Silver.

understanding

PAGE 29

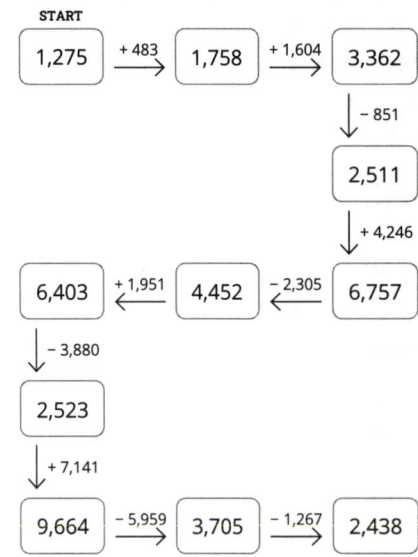

PAGE 30

a lake   a river
a walk   a village
a chomp   a shout
a cup of boiling water   a damp towel

Drawings will vary.

PAGE 31

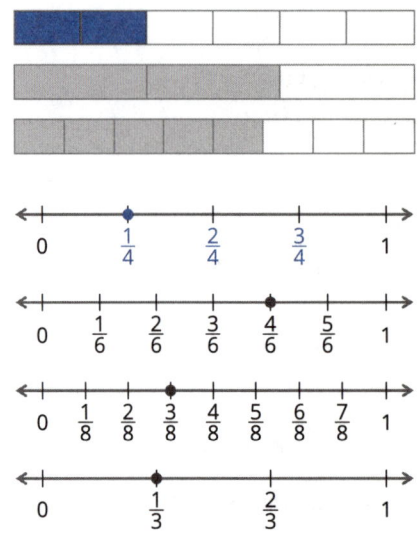

PAGE 32

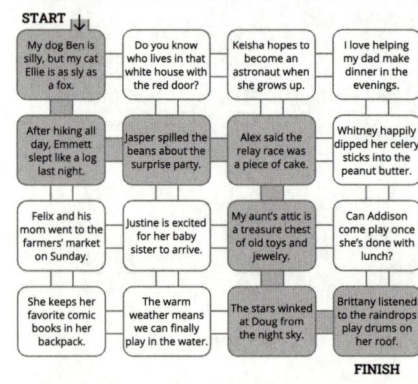

PAGE 33

makes laws for the whole United States	builds state highways	meets in the Capitol Building in Washington, D.C.
gives people driver's licenses	is sometimes led by a mayor	prints U.S. dollars
builds playgrounds in a city, town, or county	meets in a state capitol	makes laws for a city, town, or county
is led by the president	is in charge of the United States Armed Forces	is led by a governor
meets at a city hall, town hall, or county seat	makes laws for a state	collects trash from people's houses

PAGE 34

3,287 more fans

1,860 hot dogs

4,610 more fans

2,687 cups

$3,532

PAGE 35

1	3	2	5	6	8	9	4	7
6	7	5	4	9	2	3	8	1
4	8	9	3	7	1	2	5	6
9	1	8	2	5	6	7	3	4
7	5	3	9	1	4	6	2	8
2	6	4	8	3	7	1	9	5
8	2	1	7	4	9	5	6	3
3	4	6	1	2	5	8	7	9
5	9	7	6	8	3	4	1	2

PAGE 36

PR**E**SENT

PEN

BARK

Answer key

PAGE 36 (continued)

TIRE
DUCK
RULER
SPRING
CAN
LIGHT

Riddle answer: SPARKLING

PAGE 39

8	24	7
50	12	0
35	70	25
72	0	24
15	48	81
49	27	32
42	64	54

PAGE 40

Answers will vary. Some possible answers are shown below.

Recently, high winds from a storm broke the basketball hoop in our neighborhood park. To raise money for a new hoop, a group of us decided to have a yard sale. **First**, Dylan and I told our neighbor, Mr. Jordan, that we wanted to use the empty corner lot for the yard sale next Saturday. He thought our idea was great, and he even let us borrow some tables! **Now**, we need to get the word out to more people. Kayla is making signs **tonight** to inform our neighbors about the yard sale. **Tomorrow**, she will put the signs up around the neighborhood while the rest of us gather items for the yard sale. With any luck, we will **soon** raise enough money to buy a new hoop.

PAGE 41

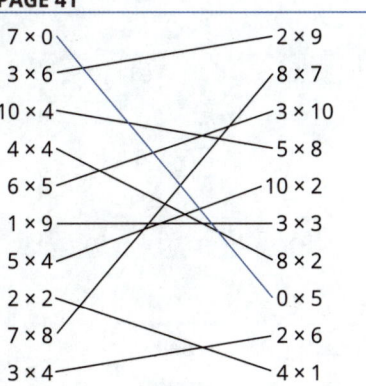

PAGE 42

Laila and Sara (gaze) | gazes at the stars in the dark night sky.

Asher practice | (practices) piano every day.

Our two orange cats (notice) | notices the birds on our back porch.

The river in the valley flow | (flows) under the old wooden bridge.

The weary travelers (settle) | settles into their rooms for the evening.

I (save) | saves all of my dad's loose change in a big glass jar.

The bakery down the street prepare | (prepares) for the morning rush.

People in the park (admire) | admires the amazing chalk artists.

Answers will vary. Some possible answers are shown below.

The train (blows) its whistle in three long, loud bursts.

We (swim) laps in the pool every day before breakfast.

The children (smile) at the thought of homemade maple pecan ice cream.

Coach Anderson (leads) the kids through the course before the race.

Daffodils (blossom) every spring in my uncle's garden.

Ms. Wilson (carves) the wood into the shape of an elephant.

PAGE 43

Rock A: sedimentary
Rock B: metamorphic
Rock C: igneous
Rock D: sedimentary
Rock E: igneous
Rock F: metamorphic

PAGE 44

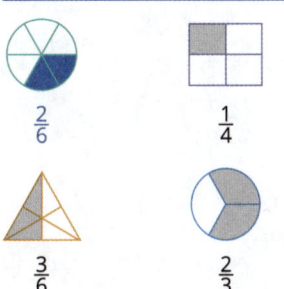

PAGE 44 (continued)

PAGE 46

Japan

square paper

Sample answer: Pressing down with a flat tool makes the folds neater and helps the design hold its shape.

to tell about special tools used in origami

simple

a stapler

PAGE 47

Answers will vary.

PAGE 48

Answers will vary.

PAGE 49

Heather likes eating peaches.

Sasha's plane will arrive on time.

Joe and Beth are building a campfire.

The strong wind blew.

Fish swim lazily in the pond.

We rode the bus to the beach.

The zipper on Aisha's green backpack broke yesterday.

My friends and I plan to start a band this summer.

Duncan will pick up veggie burgers for the cookout.

My favorite great-uncle visited us last weekend.

The summer sun peeked through the fog surrounding the mountain.

The smell of freshly baked bread drifted out from the kitchen.

Answers will vary.

Answer key

PAGE 50
15 stickers

32 pieces of pizza

42 lilies

24 seats

63 cones

PAGE 51
Answers will vary. Some possible answers are shown below.

Additionally

Afterward

As a result

For example

Therefore

Finally

First

PAGE 52

3	5	6
5	2	8
4	10	9
7	7	4
8	6	9
6	7	10
7	4	8

PAGE 54
a supply store near the Oregon Trail

Sample answer: She likes that the store is full of people getting ready to set out on the Oregon Trail. She likes to hear their stories and imagine her own adventures.

Answers will vary. Some possible answers are shown below.

	Point of view	Evidence
Lucy	Lucy believes the Oregon Trail will be an exciting adventure.	She loves listening to the travelers' stories and imagining what her own adventures will be like.
Henry	Henry believes the Oregon Trail will take him away from everything he's ever known.	He doesn't know if he wants to leave everything and everyone behind. He's worried he might get scared or lonely.

curious, adventurous, friendly

PAGE 54 (continued)
Sample answer: Henry's conversation with Lucy makes him feel more hopeful about his journey. He is less nervous about leaving and is looking forward to making new friends.

PAGE 55

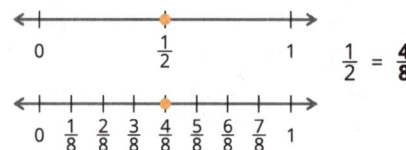

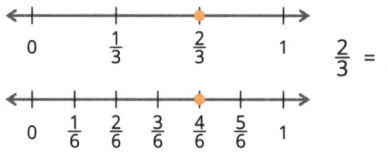

$\frac{1}{2} = \frac{4}{8}$

$\frac{2}{3} = \frac{4}{6}$

$\frac{1}{2} = \frac{2}{4}$ $\frac{2}{4} = \frac{4}{8}$ $\frac{1}{2} = \frac{3}{6}$

$\frac{1}{3} = \frac{2}{6}$ $\frac{1}{2} = \frac{5}{10}$ $\frac{3}{4} = \frac{6}{8}$

PAGE 56
Rhode Island

Arizona

Wisconsin

Kentucky

Wyoming

New Jersey

West Virginia

Michigan

Texas

Washington

Maine

North Carolina

Illinois

Montana

Alaska

Nebraska

PAGE 57

Order of performers	
1	Jin
2	Kiara
3	Liam
4	Gabe
5	Lucas
6	Mila
7	Olivia
8	Elena
9	Carlos

PAGE 58
Mars

Earth

Saturn

Mercury

Answers will vary.

PAGE 59
what time the event happened

a skateboarding trick

PAGE 60
Answers will vary. Some possible answers are shown below.

Details ONLY in the newspaper article	Details ONLY in Troy's letter
• Colorful designs were painted throughout the space. • Food trucks served hot dogs, burgers, and frozen lemonade.	• Kids traded skateboarding tips. • Troy won a new helmet.
Details in both	
• The skate park had ramps, rails, and half-pipes. • Students from the nearby skateboarding school gave free lessons.	

PAGE 61

4	×	3	=	12		
×		×		÷		
7		6	×	**6**	=	36	8
=		=		=		÷	×
28		18	÷	2	=	9	2
						=	=
				4	×	**4**	=	16
				×				
42	÷	**7**	=	6		64		21
		×		=		÷		÷
		9		24	÷	**8**	=	3
		=				=		=
		63		56	÷	8	=	7

PAGE 62
attract   repel

attract   attract

repel   attract

Answer key

PAGE 63

Tracy's
windows
rocket's
bikes
city's
children's
Pedro's
books
bakers'
girls'
rabbits

PAGE 64

28 lemons
9 packs
80 umbrellas
5 cups of water
$27

PAGE 65

buddy   scent
perfect   quick
calm   confusing

companion — a friend
ideal — the best
serene — quiet and peaceful
aroma — a pleasant smell
brisk — lively, active, or fast
perplexing — hard to understand

PAGE 66

$\frac{2}{5} < \frac{4}{5}$

$\frac{3}{6} > \frac{3}{8}$

$\frac{3}{4} > \frac{1}{4}$ $\frac{1}{8} < \frac{1}{2}$ $\frac{1}{3} < \frac{2}{3}$

$\frac{6}{10} < \frac{6}{8}$ $\frac{4}{6} < \frac{5}{6}$ $\frac{6}{8} > \frac{5}{8}$

$\frac{9}{10} > \frac{7}{10}$ $\frac{4}{5} > \frac{4}{6}$ $\frac{2}{5} < \frac{2}{4}$

PAGE 67

Answers will vary. Some possible answers are shown below.

Jackson and Jenny joyfully juggle jam jars in January.

PAGE 67 (continued)

Bobby baked big batches of bitter brown bread.

Three thousand thoughtful thinkers were thinking of how the three thieves got through.

Answers will vary.

PAGE 68

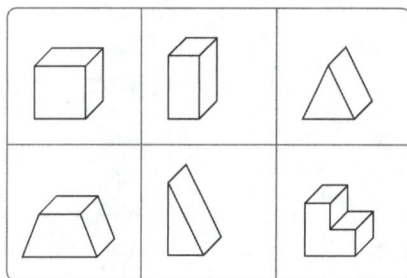

PAGE 71

18	32	14
180	320	140
1,800	3,200	1,400

48	15	36
480	150	360
4,800	1,500	3,600

21	10	30
210	100	300
2,100	1,000	3,000

560   1,600   270
160   4,500   7,200
4,200 400   3,600

PAGE 72

began
taught
lost
built
spoke
chose
thought
drove
forgot
became
wore
met

PAGE 73

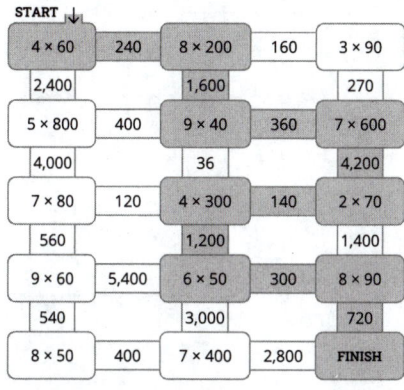

PAGE 74

Answers will vary. Some possible answers are shown below.

Human resources	Natural resources	Capital resources
• teacher	• wind	• paint brush
• author	• stone	• tractor
• scientist	• cotton	• computer
• chef	• fish	• frying pan

Answers will vary. One possible answer is shown below.

Good	Human resources	Natural resources	Capital resources
wooden table	carpenter	wood	hammer, nails
bread	baker	wheat, water	oven

PAGE 75

deer
rode
flower
find
threw
its
write
you're
aloud
scene
passed

Answers will vary. Some possible answers are shown below.

I sent a letter to my grandma.

A penny is worth one cent.

I love the scent of fresh cookies.

Answer key

PAGE 76

$\frac{3}{4} < \frac{7}{8}$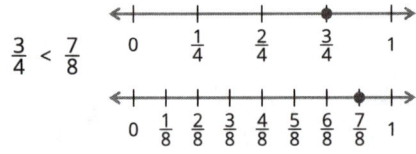

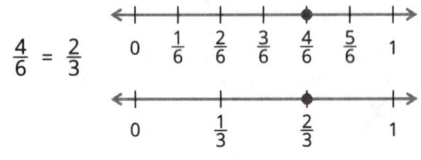

$\frac{4}{6} = \frac{2}{3}$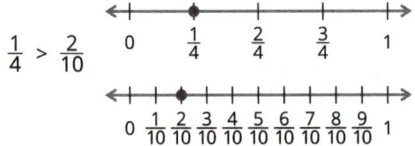

$\frac{1}{4} > \frac{2}{10}$

PAGE 78

She teaches her how to balance and choose the best rocks.

Sample answer: Elsie is frustrated but determined. She shakes off the dust from her fall and tries the climb again the next day.

Answers will vary. Some possible answers are shown below.

1.	She tests each stone before putting her full weight on it.
2.	She takes breaks to catch her breath.
3.	She stops on small ledges to rest her tired legs.

brave (helpful) daring silly (wise) selfish

Learning from your mistakes can lead to success.

high resting spot

PAGE 79

Answers will vary.

PAGE 80

Answers will vary.

PAGE 81

Sleep is the most important thing you can do for your brain.

The ukulele is the easiest instrument to learn how to play.

Everyone should read historical fiction.

PAGE 81 (continued)

The aquarium is such an interesting place to visit!

Answers will vary. One possible answer is shown below.

My bunny, Marlow, is very smart.

PAGE 82

50	70	30
60	230	200
590	740	4,850
3,720	1,920	9,270
700	900	400
300	400	600
1,000	2,700	4,300
1,200	5,500	8,200

PAGE 84

Tennessee and North Carolina

Answers will vary. Some possible answers are shown below.

Cause	Effect
Light mist and fog hanging over the mountains look like smoke.	The mountains got the name "smoky."
There is a lot of water in the air.	Plants and trees stay healthy and green.
The park is home to many types of salamanders.	The park is known as the "Salamander Capital of the World."

Answers will vary. Some possible answers are shown below.

1.	cool, damp forests
2.	clear mountain streams

Sample answer: The author thinks Great Smoky Mountains National Park is a wonderful place to visit. The author talks about the park's beauty and the many plants and animals you can see there.

PAGE 85

18 × 4 is about 20 × 4 = 80 chairs

36 × 3 is about 40 × 3 = 120 fruit chews

24 × 7 is about 20 × 7 = 140 mini muffins

182 × 3 is about 200 × 3 = 600 balloons

320 × 5 is about 300 × 5 = 1,500 tickets

PAGE 86

C	F
C	R
F	R
R	C
F	R
F	C

Answers will vary. Some possible answers are shown below.

He likes pizza, but it's not his favorite food.

My cousin adopted a dog and named her Teena.

PAGE 87

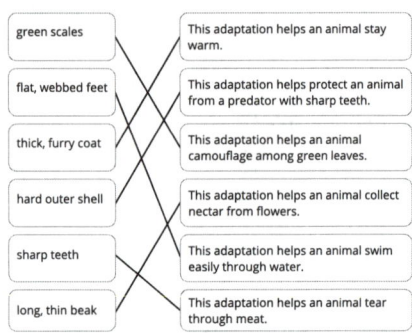

PAGE 88

18 square inches   36 square feet

20 square meters   49 square yards

48 square kilometers   72 square miles

PAGE 89

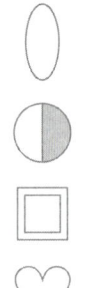

PAGE 90

Drawings will vary.

Answer key

PAGE 91

Equations may vary. Some possible answers are shown below.

6 + 40 = 46 square meters
49 + 27 = 76 square yards
18 + 12 = 30 square inches
28 + 40 = 68 square miles

PAGE 92

A   A
A   B
B   A
B   B
A   A
A   B
B   B
A   A

Answers will vary.

PAGE 93

6 × 23 = (6 × **20**) + (6 × **3**)
      = **120** + **18**
      = **138**

3 × 19 = (3 × **10**) + (3 × **9**)
      = **30** + **27**
      = **57**

5 × 17 = (5 × **10**) + (5 × **7**)
      = **50** + **35**
      = **85**

8 × 26 = (8 × **20**) + (8 × **6**)
      = **160** + **48**
      = **208**

PAGE 94

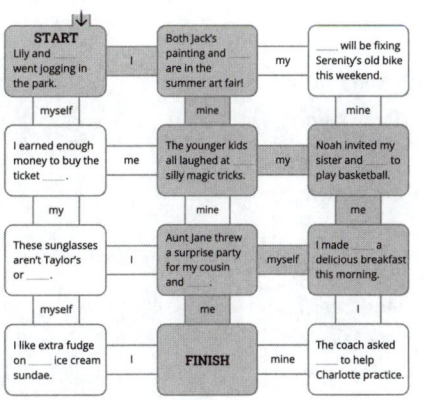

PAGE 95

Equations and models may vary. Some possible solutions are shown below.

4 × 15 = (4 × **10**) + (4 × **5**)
      = **40** + **20**
      = **60**

5 × 22 = (5 × **20**) + (5 × **2**)
      = **100** + **10**
      = **110**

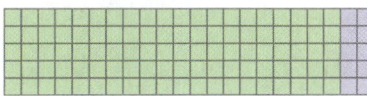

6 × 16 = (6 × **10**) + (6 × **6**)
      = **60** + **36**
      = **96**

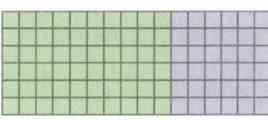

4 × 24 = (4 × **20**) + (4 × **4**)
      = **80** + **16**
      = **96**

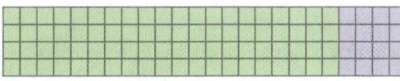

PAGE 96

Sample answer: The speaker is talking to his family. He is at home on the couch listing all of the outside activities they have done together.

Sample answer: The speaker won't go outside, even for money.

ABAB

playful

Sample answer: The words "I've had it. I'm done" and "forty-three games" create a funny tone, while the rhyme and rhythm keep the poem light and playful.

PAGE 97

Answers will vary.

PAGE 98

Martin Luther King, Jr. Memorial	Empire State Building	Mount Rushmore
Independence Hall	Capitol Building	Jefferson Memorial

PAGE 99

SUNDAY
WRONG
A FISH
THE RULER
A PALM TREE
THE LIBRARY
A GUMMY BEAR
A THESAURUS

PAGE 100

	Position				
Jersey number	Point guard	Shooting guard	Small forward	Power forward	Center
3	X	X	●	X	X
7	●	X	X	X	X
8	X	●	X	X	X
23	X	X	X	X	●
24	X	X	X	●	X

7
8
3
34
23

PAGE 103

Sample answer: It is a familiar object for readers to picture how tall a redwood is.

Sample answer: It helps readers see and compare a redwood's height to a building and a human.

by taking in water from the air

PAGE 104

Sample answer: The words are organized in alphabetical order.

Answer key

PAGE 104 *(continued)*

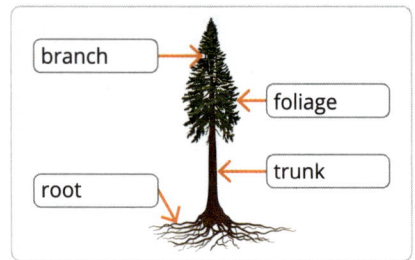

PAGE 105

4 × 23 = 92

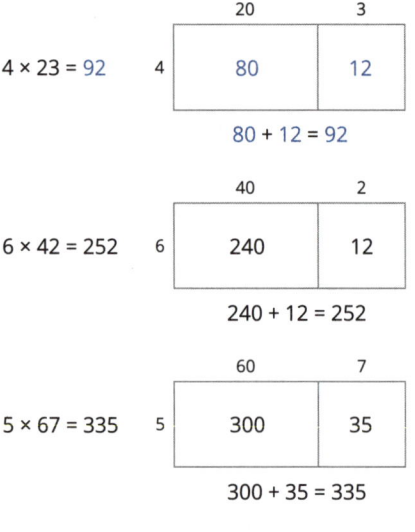

20	3
80	12

4

80 + 12 = 92

6 × 42 = 252

40	2
240	12

6

240 + 12 = 252

5 × 67 = 335

60	7
300	35

5

300 + 35 = 335

8 × 79 = 632

70	9
560	72

8

560 + 72 = 632

PAGE 106

3 × 85 = 255

80	5
240	15

3

240 + 15 = 255

7 × 94 = 658

90	4
630	28

7

630 + 28 = 658

6 × 73 = 438

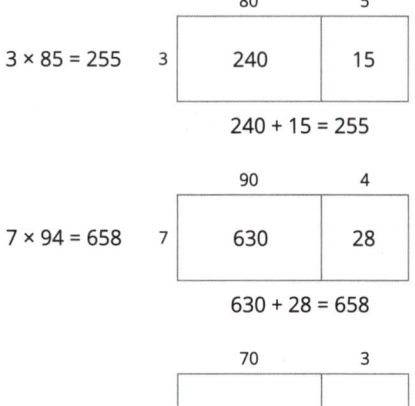

70	3
420	18

6

420 + 18 = 438

PAGE 106 *(continued)*

9 × 36 = 324

30	6
270	54

9

270 + 54 = 324

PAGE 107

Answers will vary. Some sample answers are shown below.

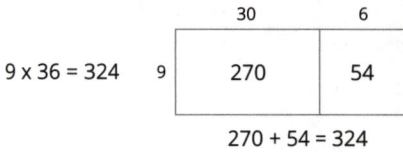

How did people keep ~~there~~ **their** homes cool before modern air conditioning**?** For thousands of years, people ~~a round~~ **around** the world have built houses out of mud to beat the heat. Mud bricks are made of earth, water, and straw. They soak up the heat of the ~~son~~ **sun**, while the inside of the building ~~stay~~ **stays** cool.

Natural caves usually stay cool, ~~to~~ **too**. In one tiny Spanish town, people ~~builded~~ **built** walls into the sides of rocky cliffs to make cave-like buildings. ~~summers~~ **Summers** are hot and dry, but the homes in the rocks stay ~~Nice~~ **nice** and cool**.**

In 1915, miners in ~~australia~~ **Australia** needed a ~~weigh~~ **way** to stay cool while searching for gold and gems. It was 120°F outside, and they found relief in the holes they dug. Soon, they turned those underground ~~wholes~~ **holes** into homes and called them dugouts**.** Even today, the dugouts stay ~~an~~ **a** lovely 75°F all year long.

PAGE 108

PAGE 109

93°F

3 days

16 days

4 more days

PAGE 110

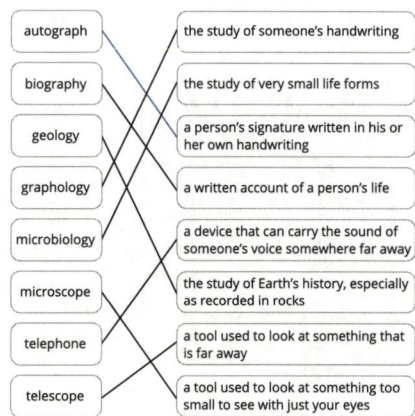

PAGE 111

wet pet
brave wave
damp camp
breeze squeeze
shell smell
whale tale
beach speech
sand band
lake cake

Answer key

PAGE 112

7	**8**	3
2	6	**10**
9	4	**5**

12	5	**10**
7	9	**11**
8	**13**	6

16	**15**	20
21	**17**	13
14	**19**	**18**

27	34	29
32	**30**	28
31	26	**33**

PAGE 113

Equations and models may vary. Some possible solutions are shown below.

201

	60	7
3	180	21

180 + 21 = 201

332

	80	3
4	320	12

320 + 12 = 332

408

	60	8
6	360	48

360 + 48 = 408

329

	40	7
7	280	49

280 + 49 = 329

648

	70	2
9	630	18

630 + 18 = 648

472

	50	9
8	400	72

400 + 72 = 472

PAGE 114

1891

1894

the NBA

45 years

The WNBA was formed.

PAGE 115

Answers will vary.

PAGE 116

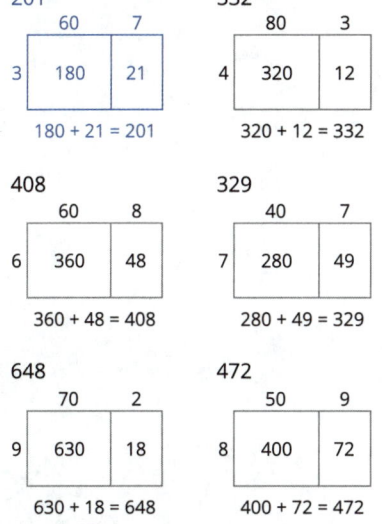

8 × 29 = 232   2 × 85 = 170   6 × 39 = 234

5 × 67 = 335   3 × 78 = 234   7 × 59 = 413

9 × 26 = 234   6 × 42 = 252   4 × 57 = 228

PAGE 117

Underlined details will vary. Some possible answers are shown below.

They found themselves surrounded by tall green columns. It was the grass, they realized after a moment.

The soccer ball is as big as a house!

Sample answer: It is probably a small animal like a cat. The title mentions a cat, and since the children are tiny now, a cat might seem as big as an elephant.

PAGE 118

S   J

J   S

Sample answer: José and Sofía learn to think before they act.

PAGE 119

4 shark teeth

$1\frac{3}{4}$ inches long

2 more shark teeth

13 shark teeth

PAGE 120

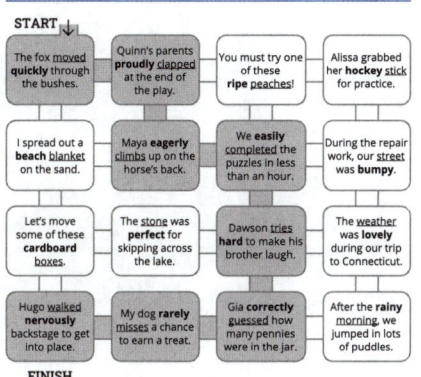

PAGE 121

palm — lamb

cedar — goat

maple — horse

lime — car

peach — plane

mango — train

golf — buns

tennis — bread

football — cupcakes

Sea animals

lobster — dolphin

coral — octopus

PAGE 122

PAGE 123

sequential

compare-contrast

descriptive

cause-effect

problem-solution

sequential

PAGE 124

sequential

compare-contrast

problem-solution

PAGE 125

72 seashells

192 pieces of taffy

$156

154 ounces

PAGE 126

Before

unless

While

since

because

As

Although

until

Answers will vary. Some possible answers are shown below.

after: We ate our sandwiches after we got to the park.

since: Since I have dance practice tonight, I can't go see the movie with you.

unless: The flowers won't grow unless they get lots of sunlight.

Answer key

PAGE 127

PAGE 128

Answers will vary.

PAGE 129

440 people

104 people

82 more people

68 dancers

24 more athletes

PAGE 130

48 pieces of candy

700 water bottles

371 pictures

139 gold balloons

PAGE 131

8 square units

2 square units

12 square units

8 square units

8 square units

38 square units

34 square units
Drawings will vary.

Answers will vary.
Drawings will vary.

PAGE 132

Answers will vary.

Certificate of Completion

Congratulations!

_____
Name

has completed this year's
Ultimate Summer Workbook
and is ready for grade 4!

_____
Date

Awarded by